BANBURY

A Century of Change

A portrait of Martin Blinkhorn, to whom this book is dedicated, the living embodiment of the business slogan 'Always carry a camera always' and someone who taught me to do the same.

BANBURY
A Century of Change

Guardian

in association with the Banbury Guardian

Brian Little

breedon books
PUBLISHING

First published in Great Britain in 2005 by

The Breedon Books Publishing Company Limited

Breedon House, 3 The Parker Centre, Derby, DE21 4SZ.

ISBN 1 85983 424 8

Printed and bound by Cromwell Press, Trowbridge, Wiltshire

CONTENTS

SKETCH MAP OF THE BOROUGH OF BANBURY, 1935

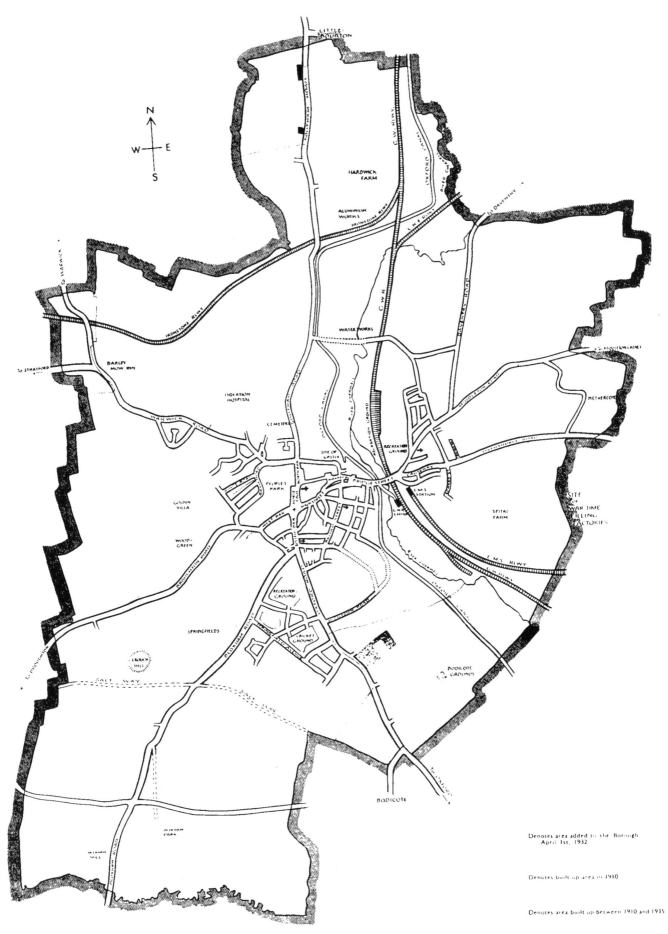

Denotes area added to the Borough
April 1st, 1932

Denotes built up area in 1910

Denotes area built up between 1910 and 1935

PREFACE

2005 is the 10th anniversary of my weekly column in the *Banbury Guardian,* and during that time it has significantly altered to take account of the growing fascination with Nostalgia. 'Look back with Little' enables readers to go back to a time when Banbury was indeed an historic market town and to learn something of the personalities who have impacted upon it. In doing so these articles have helped to reveal the town's hallmarks, which are the outward and visible signs of its 'Banburyness'.

A Century of Change is an opportunity to observe and comment on how Banbury has moved away from a world of livestock wanderings and small family shops yet delights in retaining and reviving mental images of these.

The *Guardian* is fully part of the new technological era and has its own website. At the same time the editor and her support staff have not lost sight of the importance of championing local causes, many of which relate to the increasing need to conserve our town's heritage before it vanishes in the guise of brownfield development.

INTRODUCTION

In the introduction to its early 50s town guide, E.D. Burrow observed that Banbury was 'a fascinating mixture of old and new' that had recently undergone 'something of a renaissance'. For the many who used its market town services, either by day or night, it was their kind of town with a strong local identity.

More recently a journalist working for a Sunday national newspaper has said of our town 'Nowhere is perfect – but, even so, Banbury is damn close.' The fascinating shape of the two central thoroughfares, the High Street and Parsons Street, may have influenced Sue Arnold's comment. Their alignments, parts of the mediaeval planned town, most closely resemble the letter 'S'. On the corners there are still fine buildings, none grander that the Grade II listed, half-timbered house built by Edward Vivers, who was a wealthy cloth merchant and prominent Quaker in the 17th century.

Down the years several local and national photographers have captured the features of Banbury that most convey its distinctiveness. Subsequently, these pictures were made more readily available through the medium of postcards so that generations of visitors could write those immortal words 'Wish you were here'.

At a time when Banbury is seeking to encourage a significant growth in its visitor numbers there can be no more appropriate wish. My hope is that this book will encourage visitors to stay a little while and make their own discoveries before they go in search of Cotswold villages, Shakespeare and the dreamy spires of Oxford.

ACKNOWLEDGEMENTS

For this book the principal source of photographs was the collection built up by four generations of the Blinkhorn family. I am especially indebted to Sonia Blinkhorn and her son Tom for allowing me free run of this archive.

I have also received great support from Bridget Dakin, Editor of the *Banbury Guardian*, and her staff, especially Mark Wiltshire and photographers Mike Dancer and Kirsty Edmunds.

Of course no 'Memory Lane' column could succeed without the help of its readers, and I wish to thank the following for permission to reproduce illustrations:

Mike Alcock; Sue Anker; the Armpitt Jug Band; Phyliss Arnold; Alcoa; Martin Allitt; Cecily Bailey; Banbury Choral Society; Banbury Cross Players; Banbury Historical Society; Banbury Operatic Society; Banbury School; Banbury Town Council; John Batts; the family of the late Johnny Biddle; Marjorie Bloomfield; Roger Bradshaw; Helen Brooks; Peter Buckland; John Cheney; Walter Cheney; Cherwell District Council; Richard and Margaret Clark; Dashwood Road School; John Dossett Davies; Doris Durham; Andrew Fairbairn; Derek Fairbairn; Kevin French; Jeremy Gibson; Peggy Gilbert; David Golby; Helen Hall; June Hardie; the late Charles Herbert; the late Muriel Herbert; Rosemary Higham; Anne Huggins; David Hitchcox; Stephen Jakeman; Michael Jones; Adrian Jarvis; Kraft Foods UK Ltd; Gladys Lane-Wheatcroft; Pete Lay; Malcolm Lee; Judith and George Macey; Pauline McTimony; Ray Malcolm; Les Meadows; John Perks; Rod Prewer; Photo Finish; Anne Radford; John Rakestraw; St Mary's School; Victor Side; B. Singleton; Mark Spokes; Anne Stowe; Roger Sumner; Tony Walker; the late Ernest Thrush; the Tobin family; Tudor Photography; Eddie Turvey and Caroline Winn.

Finally, my sincere thanks must go to Margaret Little, my wife, for kindly word processing the manuscript and offering a sounding board at all times.

SETTING THE SCENE
THE *BANBURY GUARDIAN* YEARS

On 5 April 1838 William Potts launched a newspaper as a way of taking the lid off the appalling conditions endured by many working-class people. It was called the *Guardian* and comprised four pages of news and advertisements.

This initiative was bold indeed as Potts published the paper at his own financial risk. However, he wanted a way of getting information to people, especially concerning workhouse conditions.

In his first leader Potts wrote 'the most essential condition to the success of the present measure (the Poor Law Act of 1833) is the election of wise and humane Boards of Guardians'. Such comment, which went to the heart of social issues, was very much a reflection of William's experience in the newspaper world. He had been correspondent on Banbury matters for the *Oxford Herald* between 1831 and 1836.

The town of Banbury, into which the *Guardian* was born, looked very different from today's built environment. Most of the houses were constructed of stone. Those in the High Street, Parsons Street and Market Place often had small shops at the front and were owned by people like Timothy Goffe, who used the medium of Potts's first issue to record 'thanks to his numerous friends, for the liberal support he has experienced during the eight years he has been in business, and hopes to receive a continuance of their favours.'

By the time issue No.2 of the *Guardian* had appeared on 3 May 1838, it had increased in size to eight pages. News continued to fill its front cover until 1839 when advertisements took over.

Potts focussed strongly on the state of housing for the working classes. He offered a prize of £3 to anyone who would send in a specification of a cottage with drainage and ventilation to a high standard that could be built at a cost not exceeding £100. A Mr Kendall of Kineton submitted an excellent design, but we do not know if he got the award.

During the 1840s hard news appeared with greater frequency, though it was more national than local. Potts did, however, record the Borough of Banbury's horror at an assassination attempt on the life of Queen Victoria.

With stories like this coming to hand it was clearly desirable to convert the newspaper into a weekly, and the *Banbury Guardian* was born on 4 July 1843.

In this first issue of the new style paper Potts set out what we would now call a mission statement: 'to give the earliest and most accurate account of all occurrences of legitimate public interest, suppressing nothing out of regard to the supposed interests of any political party.'

This reveals a very lively sense of a newspaper's obligations but these high ideals were not always adhered to. Barrie Trinder, is his book *Victorian Banbury*, records that the *Banbury Guardian* and its rival the *Banbury Advertiser* sometimes sought to avoid publishing items that aroused controversy, especially on religious matters.

Despite this, the *Banbury Guardian* was not short of local news. John Potts, who took over from his father in 1867, ensured that there was a strong focus on the locality. He appointed town and village correspondents and they contributed to a paper that was, by 1876, produced on a cylinder press and folded mechanically.

John's editorship ended in 1892 when his son William succeeded him. William was responsible for introducing mechanical typesetting in 1904. The *Banbury Guardian* was one of the first county papers to have this. Each week there was

Ted Clark unveils a Blue Plaque to the second William Potts, editor of the *Banbury Guardian* and local historian. Left to right: John Bell (chairman of the Civic Society), Hugo Brunner (Lord Lieutenant of Oxfordshire), Bridget Dakin (current editor of the *Banbury Guardian*), Ted Clark, Derek Ingram (Civic Society).

a fresh typeface and the whole production process was speeded up.

William had to contend with many problems, especially during the two world wars, that deprived him of both staff and paper. The General Strike of 1926 caused him to post news in the office windows in Parsons Street. An important innovation of this was the inclusion of football reporting. This widened the paper's appeal and had an important effect on circulation figures, which grew significantly right up until the 1950s, by which time the print run had reached almost 15,000.

Before the intervention of World War Two, William Potts recruited a young reporter by the name of Ted Clark. After a short while at the *Guardian* Ted decided to widen his newspaper contacts and seek experience with the *Western Morning News*. When war broke out Ted joined the Royal Devon Regiment and was later commissioned into the Royal Berkshires. After the war he was lured back to the *Guardian* where first he acted as advertising manager and then became editor in succession to William Potts. His leadership of the paper was outstanding, and under his guidance the *Banbury Guardian* catered for all interests including those of children in the shape of Auntie Margaret's column. It was while Ted was helmsman at the *Guardian* that he and John Cheney of the renowned printing business prepared and published William Potts's manuscript, the *History of Banbury*.

In the mid-1960s Ted Clark left the *Banbury Guardian* to become deputy editor of the *Stratford-upon-Avon Herald*. This move was a direct result of Woodrow Wyatt's incorporation of the *Banbury Guardian* into his press empire and his implementation of a range of ideas that were not compatible with Ted's editorship.

One of Wyatt's most important measures was to take the *Banbury Guardian* into the realms of publishing history when it became the first newspaper in the country to print full colour pictures.

In 1975 the paper's offices moved from their historic base in Parsons Street to the green area of South Bar. This was part of a wider movement to allow businesses to revitalise large properties that had been

Ted Clark (editor), extreme right, and his *Banbury Guardian* staff about to set off on an outing, the coach was supplied by Halls of Deddington. Note the bus is parked outside the Regal Cinema in the Horse Fair.

Ted Clark (editor) explains about the paper to Princess Alice, Duchess of Gloucester.

Celebrating 160 years of the *Banbury Guardian* – receptionists Maureen Tyrell and Elaine Varney.

home to leading Banbury families. It was while the offices were based here that the 150th anniversary of William Potts's first four-page issue was celebrated. A tabloid souvenir provided the opportunity to look back at what had made the news during the paper's lifetime to date. There was also a space in which to paint a picture of the town in 1838 with its hiring fairs and plush workshops.

In 1978 Terry Bletchly, who was then advertising manager of the *Guardian,* decided to take stock of the newspaper's readership. The findings from a sample survey of three percent of homes within a 10-mile radius of Banbury revealed that more than 80 percent of those who responded were readers of the paper. This was a pleasing outcome as the total popu-

The first Banbury Business Awards on 30 January 1997. Left to right: Murray Walker (then BBC motor racing commentator), Shaun Jardine, Paul Bithell (*Banbury Guardian* editor). Before his untimely death, Paul went on to be editor-in-chief of the *Bucks Herald, Bucks Advertiser* and the *Thames Gazette* group of newspapers.

lation of the area studied was 94,427 at that time. Back in 1946 William Potts had boasted that the *Guardian* of the day was 'the leading advertising medium and business organ in a district of 82,000 people'.

By 1998, the 160th year of publication, the paper's offices were based in North Bar next to a heritage building in the shape of the Dog and Gun, once a coaching inn. Although long since retired from the newspaper world, Ted Clark's continued interest in the paper right up to his death in 2004 encouraged him to forecast a meaningful role and prosperous future for the *Guardian*. Under the current editor, Bridget Dakin, the *Banbury Guardian* has staked its claim to care about issues that are impacting on the character and soul of the town.

THE CHANGING FACE
OF BANBURY

A pictorial map of Banbury town centre displayed outside the former White Lion Hotel.

Despite the emergence of the Cherwell area industrial suburb during the second half of the 19th century, Banbury in 1905 was still very much a country market town. This continued to be recognised by the large number of village carriers for whom Banbury was their principal metropolis. Morland's Guide to Banbury and District, published four years earlier, made a significant statement about the location of the town: 'Banbury, situated as it is amidst a network of villages is unequalled… in its advantages by any town of its size in the kingdom. The picturesqueness and beauty of the neighbourhood, together with its exceptional historical interest, render Banbury one of the most noted towns in the whole of England.'

While not seeking to disagree with this verdict, it is important to appreciate that if part of the attraction of the town was livestock wandering the streets then that image was starting to change during the period leading up to World War One. Road space was being shared with a steadily increasing number of cars and

The centre part of the High Street before World War One. The Red Lion (right) gave it character.

Church House and St Mary's Church *c.*1910.

motorcycles. Local garages such as Ewins and Pytchley Autocars, both appropriately near the Cross, were offering vehicles for hire but also the likes of 'Runabouts' and 'Touring Cars' for sale.

The other reason for a cautious approach to Morland's enthusiastic state-ment is that the Victorian era of rapidly constructed terraces had left a legacy of sub-standard property in Banbury. The town's status enabled it to attract the up and coming chain stores such as Boots and W.H. Smith. The latter started with a bookstall at the GWR railway station.

The Horse Fair – Cockhorse café and private hotel to the left of the Whately Hall Hotel in the 1930s.

West Bar/Horse Fair corner. This block replaced the County Garage.

South Bar with
Blinkhorns Photographic
Studio, extreme right,
before statues were
added to the Cross
(1914) to mark the
Coronation of George V
a few years earlier. The
railings were removed in
1927.

The Edwardian period in Banbury was a time of change as well as persistence. In the Horse Fair the north side had been occupied by elegant private houses, one at least ivy covered and thatched. In 1904, using a £3,000 legacy left to St Mary's Church by the widow of the Revd Back (a former vicar who had worked so hard to reorder the interior of the church), a committee headed by Canon Porter, the current vicar, succeeded in securing the erection of Church House on this site. Three years later the Blinkhorn family converted the former Corn Exchange on the western side of the Market Place into a picture palace. According to Thomas Ward Boss, Mechanics Institute librarian, the High Street had also altered to the extent of several new shop fronts.

Although some letters to the *Banbury Guardian* written round about the time of World War One seemed to indicate the blight of the Cherwell slums, nevertheless there were parts of the town that were a reason for pride. One of these was South Bar, where there were a growing number of retailers. The *Guardian* described the Cross end of the town as 'an attractive shopping centre'. The paper added by way of explanation that 'South Bar has increasing possibilities of being a pleasant part of the town; increased business is bound to be the experience of the future.' Someone who fervently believed this was Frederick Tyrell, who was a florist, fruitier

and seedsman at 11 South Bar. Maybe it was the embryo suburb of Easington that by the early 1920s generated a part of his custom.

South Bar and The Green were seen as appealing for other reasons. Some memories penned by Norman Scroxton, a headteacher at Grimsbury County School, highlighted the way children made full use of the wide open spaces where there was little to disturb the rhythm of street games apart from an occasional pony and trap or waggonnette and the even rarer motor car such as Thomas and Norman Blinkhorn's 1912 Darracq.

The special character of The Green depended on the Georgian and Victorian mansions facing on to it. Midland Marts Ltd sale catalogues of the early 1960s provide good descriptions of Linden House and No 45. Both had been high-class residences with fine rear gardens. Within its high walls the latter had formal and vegetable gardens with ornamental ponds, shrubs and trees, fruit bushes and fruit trees as well as an asparagus bed.

By the time of these sales the business potential of properties in the Cross area was starting to be realised. Occupation by the likes of solicitors and management consultants was the best hope for the care of buildings within a conservation zone. For a brief while a day nursery organisation exploited the size of one of these houses; perhaps not such a surprising

A 1950s view of the west side of The Green when some of the properties were still in private ownership.

Linden House – a fine Georgian house on The Green. Today it is part of a Business Zone.

development as back in the 1920s a dame school had appeared on The Green.

After World War One, with the return to civilian life of the town's surveyor Sidney Hilton, a new corner of Banbury took shape. This was Easington, which the *Banbury Guardian* described as 'a little known district'. Interestingly, Banbury Harriers Athletic Club's new home (now the site of Harriers Ground Primary School) was on the edge of this district but announced itself as offering 'a splendid view over the surrounding country'. As for

the houses beyond, the Revd A.L.E. Williams (Vicar of Banbury) remarked with confidence that it was 'a great new residential suburb'. He went on to refer to well-kept streets such as Springfield Avenue and Easington Road, a few necessary shops like that of Mr Harris the baker, a recreation ground and a magnificently equipped secondary school (Banbury County School) but regretted the lack of space for worship or indeed a public hall.

The vicar's hopes were realised in 1933

Miss Winter's School at 51 The Green reveals a delightful rear garden with a mulberry tree – a reminder of times past. Back row, left to right: Miss Spencer, Peter Mackay, Euan Pritchard, Margery Pursaill (married Charles Lester), unknown, Roy Booth (son of Capt Booth, builder), Edwin Bennett (son of H.O. Bennett, knitted goods manufacturer), unknown. Front row: Kathleen Peet (parents managed Warwick Road Workhouse), Keith Booth (brother of Roy), Joan Mander (daughter of a bank manager), Denis Deveen, Phyllis Bennett (sister of Edwin), Barry Deveen, Miss Rymer.

Len Withey's Easington Dairy in Horton View. This was also the first location for the Easington sub-Post Office.

The Golden Villa in 1920s. Today this building is surrounded by the Bretch Hill estate.

when St Hugh's Church Hall opened in Ruskin Road. It was not long before this Anglican place of worship was at the centre of major events such as dances and summer fetes, although most of the latter were held in Springfield School grounds off Bloxham Road.

Despite the existence of 372 houses in the Easington of 1928, it took a further year before Banbury's mayor, Councillor Mascord, opened Hunt Edmunds Easington Hotel. The brewery secured a licence by closing the Fox tavern in the Market Place. This inspired Colonel Stockton to remark that 'now the Fox had broken cover and come out he was certain there would be an enormous field on his tail'. A significant expansion of Easington occurred in the 1950s when local builders Timms's Oxford Road estate took shape and the whole of Easington was given a boost by the completion of Queensway a

little later, enabling it to take on its role as part of the town's inner ring road.

Major expansions of the town towards the north and west did not come about until the 1950s and 1960s. Some employees of the Northern Aluminium Company had started this process in the 1930s and occupied property in the likes of Ruscote Avenue, but real catalysts were two separate overspill agreements: the first with London County Council in 1952 and then with Birmingham in the mid-1960s. The latter followed the arrival of Alfred Bird and Sons, the custard and coffee manufacturers. Families from London formed an important nucleus on the Council-owned Bretch Hill estate. Land acquisition for this began in the late 1940s and diminished the area's emphasis on farming. Bird's folk were more scattered but many were housed in villages close to Banbury such as Middleton

Thomas Deely's cart in the
Market Place near the Fox
beerhouse, on the left.

A typical Bretch Hill farm. This one is attached to the Golden Villa.

A view of Bretch Hill estate in 1966 with Bird's coffee plant in the centre background. These houses were built on land belonging to the four farms that occupied the Bretch.

Cheney, but, significantly, as far as the town was concerned there were new developments north of the Warwick Road as well as executive-style housing in areas such as Poets Corner just off the Bloxham Road expanding the town westward.

In contrast to this growth, the town virtually lost a suburb in the 1960s. Slum clearance of the Cherwell terraces meant the end of former lively and closely-knit communities with their associated beer houses such as the Bird in Hand and the Chequers. Apart from the age of property, this area had never really recovered from the closure of Samuelson's Britannia Works in 1931.

In the early 21st century Banbury's north-west frontier continues to edge outwards. Hardwick and now Hanwell Fields are the manifestations of this trend but the underlying reasons are no longer the same. Cherwell District Council has had and continues to have a commitment

Manor Farm House, a 17th-century Horton stone gem on Grimsbury's rapidly changing northern boundary.

to Central Government demands for a share of the county's new housing development. House builders have taken up the

Upper Windsor Street in the mid-1960s.

Hanwell fields housing mix with a small play area.

challenge but have become conscious of the need to create distinctive physical and social environments in the areas between town and country. The same process, though, with a possible M40 motorway influence, has led to considerable growth on the northern and eastern fringes of Grimsbury. Meanwhile, the real battle zone has switched to the eastern margin of Bodicote. Here plateau land high up above the Cherwell valley has been earmarked for about 1,100 new homes. Village residents with some support from Banbury estates like Cherwell Heights and Bodicote Chase have opposed the plans with vigour, viewing the site as town overspill and a threat to the continued separate identity of Bodicote.

Another facet of the changing face of Banbury has been the development and likely future development of blocks of apartments on brownfield sites such as in Britannia Road, where the former Spencer factory was recently demolished, in the Warwick Road close by the North Bar box junction and where Hartford Motors has turned into Clark's Court.

Threats to property that is historically significant but not necessarily protected by designated area or listed status have inspired groups of interested people to go out and plot the town's character areas in the wake of proposals to extend the Conservation Zone. Articles in the *Banbury Guardian* have highlighted the issues and ensured that there has been press and public support for the efforts to retain vital elements of traditional and characteristic Banbury landscapes.

In 2005 the *Country Life* magazine mounted a search for favourite market towns. Its editor predicts a renaissance for

A grand firework
display to mark the
renovation of
Grimsbury Manor.

Spencer House – how it used to look.

Demolition reveals the interior design of Spencer's work areas.

A last look through the arch (former entrance) reveals modern flats and the spire of Marlborough Road Methodist Church.

such places. Despite signs in Banbury's urban fringe that remind the motorist of the approaching historic market town, the loss of the livestock market in 1998 much reduced vibrancy for the produce markets, and the continuing disappearance of period buildings and a further decline in small family shops have all necessitated the search for a new future, based perhaps on tourism. Visitors will be drawn to the shopping attractions of Castle Quay, while industry's new directions point to motor sport and distribution-based businesses especially. It is hoped that the unveiling of the Lady on the White Horse, highlighting Banbury's connection with the world famous nursery rhyme, in April 2005 will give a valuable boost to both visitor numbers and to the future of retail businesses located towards the Cross end of the town.

Peoples Place apartments in North Bar in 2005. On the opposite corner by the lights is the Three Pigeons. The original inn was built in 1705 and substantially rebuilt c.1910.

Bridge Street before the redevelopment. A bus (centre background) is turning into Castle Street, probably to enter the bus station.

Castle Quay takes shape close to Concorde Avenue (inner relief road).

RUNNING THE TOWN

In 1905 the administration of local government matters, including elementary education, was in the hands of a Town Council, which since 1889 had been made up of 6 aldermen and 18 councillors. The aldermen were Messrs T.O. Hankinson (pork butcher), W.R. Cooper, W.H. Walkley, H.R. Webb, A. Fairfax (solicitor) and J.J. Chard (landlord of the Reindeer). Among the councillors were some very well known and respected people: W.L. Whitehorn, W.J. Bloxham, W. Hefford, A.J. Kilby, J.T. Mawle and H. Boxold.

They supported and had oversight of officials such as Oliver James Stockton (town clerk) and J.P. Gillett (treasurer). Among these appointments were some for roles that either do not exist today or do not exist in the same mode. There was a Collector of Stallage (dues from the erection of market stalls), a manager for the Borough's Pinhill Farm (long built upon) and an Inspector of Nuisances and Canal Boats.

William Potts, in his *Banbury through One Hundred Years* (published 1942), reckoned that by that time the work of the Borough Council had more than doubled. On one front alone a series of housing acts

since 1914 had required considerable attention to their implementation.

It came as no surprise in 1932 when the council made the post of town clerk full time. Ernest Owen Reid, a solicitor who had previously worked for Coventry Council, was appointed. This was exactly two years after the purchase by the borough of the old County School premises in Marlborough Road. These became the municipal offices and a new Council Chamber was duly created to replace the outgrown facilities in the Town Hall.

Until 1945 elected representative on Banbury Borough Council were responsible for whole town matters. After this, sub-division of the town into area wards meant that those people who gained most votes at elections had to show some interest in the particular problems and issues of the parts of the town they represented, such as Easington and Grimsbury.

Throughout the hundred years covered by this book it has never been easy to stir the political blood of electors. In 1937 out of an electorate of 7,690 people only 38 percent of these bothered to vote. Presiding officers were not exactly overworked at the polling stations, which were

John Cheney visits the 1937 coronation celebrations in Calthorpe Street.

Dashwood School, St Leonard's School, the Town Hall, Young's Garage (Warwick Road) and Banbury County School. This was the mayoral year of John Cheney and was notable for the local implications of the Coronation of George VI and for the visit of the Oxfordshire Agricultural Show.

There were the names of some equally important local businessmen and shopkeepers on the rest of the voting paper. Benjamin Allsopp was a cycle agent at 21 Bridge Street. As mayor in 1933, he had concerned himself with inter-civic visits.

Theo Clark was the flour miller in Station Approach. A Baptist, he became chairman of Banbury Spencer FC Supporters Club and president of the Banbury Cricket and Sports Club in the late 1930s (one of his twin sons, Ted Clark, later became a distinguished editor of the *Banbury Guardian*).

Sidney Ewins was a major garage proprietor who was very active in the early days of the Banbury Rotary Club and a member of the Madrigal and Glee Club.

John Arthur Deacon took over the Fox chain of chemists in 1912 and was a founder member of the Banbury Cricket and Sports Club.

The remaining candidates were Thomas Haddon (Bodicote Grange dairyman), William Mascord (carpenter and joiner), Fred Mold (market gardener) and Major Wise (chartered surveyor).

Between the time of this election and Festival of Britain year (1951), Banbury Borough Council presided over a town that grew in size from some 13,000 to about 19,000. Thereafter, and until the end of its life on 31 March 1974 under local government reorganisation, the Council's affairs were very much dominated by the consequences of two overspill agreements with the London and

Dedication of the new St John ambulance outside the Whately Hall Hotel in the Horse Fair. Top picture, left to right: unknown, Dr Gardiner Hill, The Mayor and Mayoress (1938–39 Councillor and Mrs Horace Lester), Col H. du C. Norris, Revd A.L.E. Williams (vicar of Banbury).

The Mayor, Alderman R.B. Miller, the recorder and councillors outside the Town Hall *c.*1941.

Alderman Margaret Johnson at the Mayor-making ceremony at Banbury Town Hall on 21 May 1958. Malcolm Spokes (right) has just handed over the chain of office on completion of his year as Mayor.

Birmingham authorities. Re-housing of people from these huge city regions and the establishment of associated industries were major preoccupations for officers and councillors alike.

Under the reorganisation of 1974, Banbury became part of Cherwell District Council. This body absorbed the Borough of Banbury, Banbury Rural District, Bicester Urban District and Ploughly

Banbury Mayor, Alderman Mrs Margaret Johnson, looks on as the Queen signs the visitors' book on 8 April 1959.

Crowds line the route taken by the Queen on her only visit to Banbury in 1959.

ROYAL VISIT

OF

HER MAJESTY

THE QUEEN

to

OXFORDSHIRE

Wednesday, 8th April, 1959

SOUVENIR

PROGRAMME

Rural District, giving it a southern boundary with the City of Oxford.

On 1 April 2000 Banbury acquired its first directly elected Town Council for 26 years. With 22 councillors, the Town Council provides a forum for local issues, many of which then have to be determined by Cherwell District Council. From the ranks of these councillors, a Town Mayor is elected who has a busy year of civic engagements. Some relate to established traditions, others to the relatively new, notably the now annual Cockhorse Festival that coincides with Mayor's Sunday.

A souvenir programme of the royal visit to Oxfordshire. Although Prince Philip's photograph appears on the cover, he did not accompany the Queen on this occasion.

FROM VILLAGE CARRIER TO M40 MANIA

Village carriers and buses

As mentioned in the introduction, at the outset of the century of change, 1905–2005, Banbury was the metropolis for village carriers with their carts. Their names and where they came from are listed in James Rusher's commercial directory. Some made daily journeys but many favoured Thursday, market day for both the produce and livestock. All provided the people of the villages they served with the opportunity to come into town or

In the early years of the 20th century village carriers had an annual gathering to find the carrier of the year. Both the Horse Fair (as here) and The Green were used.

Waggon and Horses (now the Banbury Cross) in Butchers Row had a roomy yard for carriers' carts. It is pictured here in the early 1930s when the landlord was J.T. Holland Griffiths. Note the wall plaques for RAC and National Cyclists Union. The lamp bears the legend 'Commercial Hotel Phone 172'.

Carriers' bells.

enabled them to order or receive goods from the shops. These could be items gathered by the carrier from a list provided by the customer or purchases pre-ordered and entrusted to the carrier by retailers.

Village carriers developed important links with inns in Banbury because of the need for food and water for their horses. A roomy yard and a genial mine host ensured that favourite venues were the White Hart, Old George, Wagon and Horses, Catherine Wheel, Windmill, Reindeer, Plough, Bear, Angel and Leathern Bottle.

It was never a comfortable journey but few carriers could have been as unlucky as Mr F. Franklin of Chipping Norton as reported in the *Banbury Guardian* of 22 June 1905. 'When about a mile from the town [Banbury], a pin of the shafts fell out letting them down, and as they struck the legs of the horse it was frightened and became restive. Mr Franklin jumped from the cart to go to the horse's head and slipped and put his ankle out.'

The few passengers who were able to ride in the carts must have had a slow and tedious journey. Their return home would not have been until late afternoon but at least the experience was a way of breaking out of the routine of village life.

Typical of those carriers who came from the fringes of Banbury's area of influence was Richard Matthews of Brailes. In 1910 he acquired the business that had been developed by the Godson family. The horse-drawn carts were by that time over 70 years old. Alfred Woodward's book, *Memories of Brailes*, contains a vivid description of these. On one occasion 'the inside of the van was almost filled, on the top there was a layer of butter flats and half-pot hampers of eggs. On the front seat by the driver was an ox hide. At the back were similar goods, which included sheepskins from local butchers.'

After World War

Plackett, a carrier based at Adderbury, one of a number of carriers who developed a bus service after carting days.

Matthews of Brailes lines his coach up behind Tanner of Sibford Gower in Bridge Street in the mid-1960s.

One Richard was joined by his son, Harold. Together they scrapped the old Godson vans and cart and by late 1923 had introduced the first of their many petrol and diesel coaches. This Ford vehicle carried the name Richard Matthews and Son. It was purchased from Lucketts of Shennington, cost £47 10s 0d (£47.50) and was painted in a distinctive olive green with black trimming. Thereafter, most buses were Bedfords, two of which were supplied by Charles Ewin whose garage was near the Cross.

The tickets issued to passengers were unusual in one very striking respect. In place of the more usual advertisements there was a verse from the Holy Bible, in fact from St Paul's epistle to the Philippians.

Although the family issued printed timetables for regular journeys, more characteristic of a small local firm was the sight of Harold on his knees in front of his house as he chalked on to a large blackboard a few of his forthcoming seaside trips or the mystery tours he ran during the summer months. Harold Matthews's coaches were also among the many to be found in the parking areas outside the Northern Aluminium works at Banbury. He conveyed workers to and from the factory for close on 40 years.

Many other carriers associated with villages in the Banbury area followed the example set by the Matthews family and began operating buses. However, from the autumn of 1919 their supremacy was substantially challenged by the Birmingham Motor Express Company Ltd, who opened a Banbury garage in Canal Street for two buses, which were used on daily services to Deddington, Hook Norton,

An early Midland Red bus with pneumatic tyres photographed in Bodicote.

Chipping Norton, Brackley, Byfield and Shipston-on-Stour. These early vehicles of the 1920s had distinctive characteristics: pneumatic tyres, high seating capacity, lightweight construction and, above all, exceptional reliability.

By 1921 the network had been widened to include Bicester, Gaydon, Kineton, Warwick, Leamington Spa, Stratford-on-Avon, Buckingham and Woodstock. The consequence of this was an increase in the number of buses based at Banbury and so

Sumner's bus stuck in snow – many villages relied of this service for work and shopping.

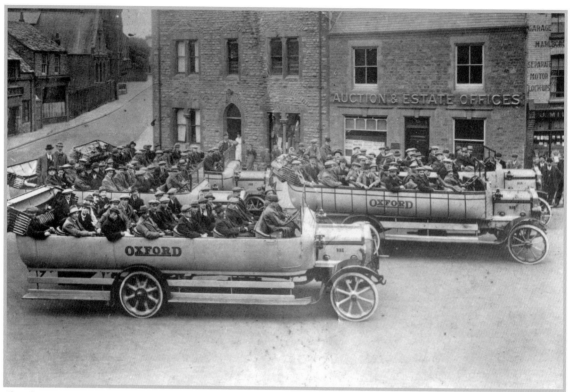

Charabanc outings were very popular in the 1920s. These City of Oxford vehicles were caught on camera outside Midland Marts office in the High Street at its junction with Marlborough Road.

The Northern Aluminium Company in 1952. The end of a shift and fleets of buses wait to take workers home.

a new and larger garage was opened to house them. With town expansion in the late 1920s and early 1930s came the growth of distinctive suburbs such as Easington, and so dedicated bus services were needed for local routes served by what is now known as the Midland Red.

Some routes out of Banbury had a special and seasonal popularity, probably because comparatively few people had their own transport in the 30s. During the summer and on Sundays charabancs ran to Edgehill, which were hugely supported by chapel folk and their children. Equally popular was an evening service to Chipping Norton that made it possible to get off and enjoy a drink in Bloxham or at the Masons Arms beyond South Newington.

Banbury Fair was an occasion for service specials. These brought people in from the villages, most of whom wanted to return by a certain time so duplication was necessary.

As for many of the village operators, work specials were very busy, especially those destined for the Northern Aluminium Company (later Alcan). These served all shifts, even the workers who clocked on at 5am.

There were also additional buses for people who wanted to experience Christmas attractions like the Leamington Spa lights. Midweek and Saturday specials enabled people from the Banbury area to enjoy spectacular displays in the Spa's gardens.

The company's 1938 booklet setting out conditions of service reveals the interesting information that drivers had to be at least 25 years of age, whereas the collection of fares could be undertaken by anyone over 21. Those behind the wheel wore brown uniforms, whereas conductors appeared in

blue and had to issue tickets of countless values, which demanded racks not provided by the company. However, a local initiative by Berry Austin in 1934 overcame this problem and was dependent on resources obtained from Hoods the ironmongers. He embedded springs from mousetraps within a suitably weighted oblong of wood.

Periodically, throughout the history of Midland Red in Banbury, the company has introduced new services that have had greater than usual significance for the local population. For instance, in February 1950 a B14 route was opened up linking Banbury with Overthorpe via the Causeway in Grimbury. Five buses each way ran on Thursdays and Saturdays, but especially valuable was a chance for people to attend the early evening house at the cinema and then to go home on the 8.12pm service. Twenty-six years later Banbury became a stopping point on an X59 service that linked Coventry with Oxford.

It was about this same time in 1976 that Leyland Nationals were introduced into North Oxfordshire. A far cry from those ground breaking vehicles of the early years, these Nationals were a joint venture by Leyland and the National Bus Company, and they replaced the double-deckers that had been a familiar sight in Banbury since the early 1960s.

That same year of 1976 also saw a reversal of what had happened in the 1920s and early 1930s, namely the withdrawal of buses from some places. Williamscot, Upper Wardington, Wardington and Chipping Warden quietly slipped out of the published timetables, and the familiar red buses no longer picked up

Sacks of letters to be dispatched via Merton Street station *c.*1905. In late Victorian and Edwardian times the railways handled substantial quantities of mail.

Most of the present day services of the Banbury area are operated by Stagecoach, and the last vehicle link with the former Midland Red Company has been severed with the withdrawal in October 2004 of Leyland Olympian (C963 XVC). During its operational days, especially on the Stratford schools run, this had symbolised just how far public transport on the roads has come since the days of pneumatic tyres.

Railways

In 1905 Banbury was pivotally placed within an extensive railway network. Information about the rail connections was locally and readily accessible within the pages of Cheney's Railway guides, which continued to be available until 1923 when a fire at the firm's printing works in Calthorpe Street ended its publication.

The era of the minibus has arrived in Banbury. Mr Bayliss (Midland Red manager), left, and Councillor Brent Prestidge (chairman of Cherwell District Council) launching the service from Bridge Street.

Eddie Turvey, a very popular long service driver with Midland Red and Stagecoach.

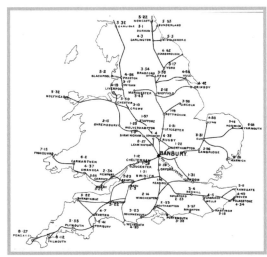

Banbury had become an important rail centre by 1901.

those who had previously waited at Charlton's the Bell, Evenley turn and Shalstone village.

On the positive side, Banbury's growing suburban tentacles were starting to determine the re-orientation of certain routes. Drivers to and from Chipping Norton had to adjust to approaching Banbury along roads bearing the names of famous poets.

Perusal of the guides reveals that travellers to London had no fewer than four routes to choose from, including the so-called 'new route'. This had opened in 1902 and provided an express corridor via Bicester and Princes Risborough. The

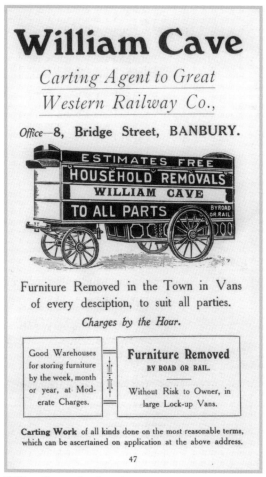

William Cave

Carting Agent to Great Western Railway Co.,

Office—8, Bridge Street, BANBURY.

ESTIMATES FREE
HOUSEHOLD REMOVALS
WILLIAM CAVE
TO ALL PARTS
BY ROAD OR RAIL

Furniture Removed in the Town in Vans of every desciption, to suit all parties.

Charges by the Hour.

Good Warehouses for storing furniture by the week, month or year, at Moderate Charges.	**Furniture Removed** BY ROAD OR RAIL. Without Risk to Owner, in large Lock-up Vans.

Carting Work of all kinds done on the most reasonable terms, which can be ascertained on application at the above address.

47

William Cave, a local carting agent.

alternatives were the Great Western line by way of Oxford, the Great Central connection via Woodford Halse and the London and North Western route into Euston. Only the GCR had no Sunday services. In addition, Banbury had connections into east Gloucestershire along the Cheltenham line.

Within the town's catchments were stations that do not exist today – Chacombe, Cropredy, Fenny Compton, Aynho, Aynho Park Platform, Adderbury, Bloxham and Hook Norton.

The guide to services in 1923 indicates stopping trains along the Great Central line that offered a service to Banbury for people who lived in places like Chacombe. Curiously, the stop there was listed as Chalcombe. Residents of the village had a choice of six trains into Banbury and seven back. On weekdays one could arrive as early as 8.07am, and the last train back departed the GWR station at 8.00pm.

By the time of the 1911 coronation, the railway companies were taking note of local events and the need for related arrangements. Typical occasions were the Crouch Hill Steeplechases and the Michaelmas Fair. Those people wishing to travel to Banbury could take advantage of cheap fares. These ranged from 7d (3p) return if you boarded at Adderbury, Cropredy and Kings Sutton to 1s 6d (7p) return from Southam Road.

Christmas has often been synonymous with having a break away from Banbury. A day in London was an opportunity to try an Express Corridor Excursion operating on the line via Bicester and Princes Risborough that had opened in 1902. There was also a lot of support for inexpensive trips to Newbury for the steeplechases.

So far as the stations were concerned, Banbury's Merton Street resembled little more than a large shed. Here, life was very leisurely except on market days. Professor Margaret Stacey, who wrote a sociological study of the town called *Tradition and Change*, based on research carried out just after World War Two, recalled sharing a compartment with livestock. The only other really busy times occurred on Saturdays, when some passengers were cinema goers, and over the three days in October, when an important boost to trade was the annual pilgrimage to Banbury Fair.

Back at the time of World War One, increased traffic of a different kind had been seen on the London and North

Memories of steam at Merton Street station.

Banbury station in 1935.

Western Railway line provided by the near location of the National Filling Factory. Large quantities of shells had to be moved and this called for a support railway system. Within the site there were no less than three miles of track, over which saddle tanks John and Lidban chugged busily back and forth.

Until reconstruction during the period 1956 to 1958, the Great Western station had a very distinctive style with its inverted 'V' roof, interior bridge for passengers to reach the London side and a number of very tall chimneys. Stories abound about people whose task it was to light and stoke the fire that ensured winter warmth for the likes of the ticket clerks.

The station changed in the mid-1950s and lost some of its charm when concrete took over. Bays were added and, from one of these, 1960s students of the North

Oxfordshire Technical College and School of Art noisily occupied autocars that conveyed them back to Bicester and Princes Risborough.

The 'Micheline', an interesting rail experiment.

By the time these students were part of the travelling public, this former Great Western station was no longer so intensively manned. During the inter-war years employment levels had peaked at a figure in excess of 200, and that did not include those who worked in the sheds or on the locomotives. Some of these employees had wider interests within Banbury, and analysis of the 1924 borough election reveals that the list of Labour candidates included two engine drivers and a plate-layer – all three came bottom of the poll. By contrast, Fred Revening, who was Great Western stationmaster at Banbury, stood as a Conservative and only missed electoral success by a few hundred votes.

The station and its train movements evoke much nostalgia for many people. There were the voices of the man who stood with his tray of Banbury cakes and of station announcer George Beddow whose helpful remarks would draw attention to where passengers might find seats on incoming services. In the declining days of steam it was still a stirring sight if you spotted a 73 Squadron locomotive leading

Waiting for the train at Banbury – 1930s style.

The Duke of Edinburgh at Banbury Station on Wednesday 6 November 1957. The occasion was an informal visit to the Northern Aluminium Company works to watch the manufacture and testing of aluminium. He met just retired Mr Duncan, who said that he would enjoy life in Banbury not his native Liverpool. 'Banbury can't be so bad then' joked the Duke.

the Leeds to Poole train. Even the diesel replacement era had its moments, as when the emergency engine happened to be called 'Victim Support'!

Now that Chiltern Turbos and Virgin Voyagers dominate train life at Banbury station, it is worth recalling a brief period in 2002 when Virgin Trains experimented with a Window Gazer's Guide to the Brighton service. Its contents revived memories of much earlier location awareness. The compiler of the Banbury section focussed on the Cross and the delightful myth about Celia Fiennes as the Lady on the White Horse.

The Oxford Canal

During the second half of the 19th century the competition between the canal and the railways was about the battle for freight, especially coal. Increasingly, fuel merchants opted to have yards where they could be serviced by rail wagons. In the early 20th century some Warwickshire coal continued to travel to the Banbury area by narrow boat, and even as late as the 1960s a dairy on the west bank of the canal still relied on this waterway. By that time, however, pleasure cruising was dominating the nature of traffic.

The popularity of this activity had been

The Corporation Yard and stores, a hive of canalside activity.

given a valuable boost by Tom Rolt and his wife in 1939 when their boat Cressy was a familiar sight following a fitting out by Tooleys at their Banbury boatyard. Together with a subsequent book entitled *Narrow Boat,* the Rolts's pursuits led to the formation of the Inland Waterways Association.

World War Two saw an increase in the use of the canal for non-perishable cargoes and especially coal. This may explain the occasional bomb such as the one in September 1940 at Banbury lock near Field's Mill and another that hit a wharf yard close to derelict buildings. A very different hazard was extreme winter

weather. The Ministry of War deployed two ice tugs in the battle to avoid delays to coal movements. Other appropriate action by the Ministry was the training of boat women to take over from men called up for active service. In his book about the Oxford Canal, Hugh Compton recalls that a Susan Woolfitt was one of the earliest females to become involved.

In the 1950s a crisis loomed for the Oxford Canal. On a July evening in 1955 people in Banbury were exhorted to join a protest meeting at the Town Hall and meet Sir A.P. Herbert and Mr R. Hickman, founder and vice-president of the Inland Waterways Association. Above all, it was the opportunity to hear Chuter Ede, a former Home Secretary. Over 300 people listened to his argument that the case for keeping canals open had never been properly debated in the House of Commons. Ede was confident that waterways could be brought up to continental standards.

During the evening many telling points were made by speakers. One noted that before nationalisation in 1947 the Oxford Canal Company had paid a four percent dividend. Another warned that local authorities could find themselves bearing the cost of infill if the canal were to be

Boats like these are very typical of Oxford Canal navigation.

Pleasure craft on the Oxford Canal line up close to Morse Marine Yard. On the left is the former bus station. The Castle Shopping Centre is in the centre in the background.

closed. Above all, there was agreement that the Oxford Canal was one of the most beautiful in England. Increasing numbers of people in pleasure craft were

The Canal Festival, an established and popular event.

discovering this fact. Their ranks had grown from 600 in 1947 to 6,000 in 1955.

Ultimately, British Waterways did not pursue the issue of closure, and an early 1970s exhibition at Banbury museum called 'Along the Cut' generated a lot of interest in the history and leisure potential of the canal.

Recent improvements to all aspects of the waterway north of the rail bridge at Banbury have played a significant part in further increases in pleasure craft. Revival of boat repair in a re-vamped Tooleys Yard, the development of the nearby Castle Quay shopping centre on a regional scale and the relocation of Banbury Museum and associated Tourist Information have been major factors in the enhancement of the attractiveness of the canal. An annual Canal Day in October is symptomatic of the realisation that the Oxford Canal is an important part of the area's future and economy.

Road Transport

The history of roads and associated traffic also reveals many highs and lows. Their condition locally was the subject of a number of letters written to the *Banbury Guardian* in January and February 1901, penned by G. Miller. In his whimsical way he assessed the situation very succinctly: 'Banbury no doubt was, in the old Midland dialect, a very picturesque town then with its old houses and countrified appearance; but though it was pleasant to the eye, it was nearly as trying to the feet as the hard peas were to the monks of old.' The Daventry Road exemplified the condition of many roads and lanes where ruts caused the Vicar of Chacombe to dismount and lead his horse to the opposite side.

Despite these concerns, by the 1920s there was a significant growth of motor traffic in the Banbury area. As a consequence local garages increased in number and business. Sidney Ewin developed close to the present Cross and set up roadside pumps in the Horse Fair. Additionally, he had a service workshop at the top of Marlborough Place, which became known as Marlborough Mews. The address suited the business because, like another garage propri-

etor, Ewin's garage grew out of a horse and carriage dealership started in 1897, the year of Queen Victoria's Diamond Jubilee. More than 40 years later the firm was official repairer to both the AA and the RAC.

As early as the 1930s Ewin found

Charles Herbert's father (right) working on West Bar pavement in the 1920s.

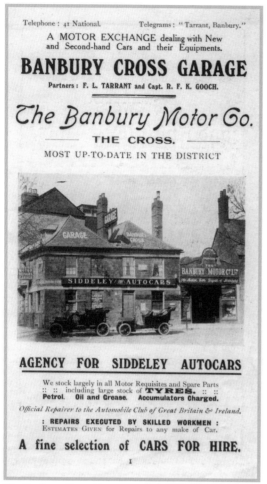

Telephone : 41 National.   Telegrams : "Tarrant, Banbury."

A MOTOR EXCHANGE dealing with New
and Second-hand Cars and their Equipments.

BANBURY CROSS GARAGE

Partners : F. L. TARRANT and Capt. R. F. K. GOOCH.

The Banbury Motor Co.

THE CROSS.

MOST UP-TO-DATE IN THE DISTRICT

AGENCY FOR SIDDELEY AUTOCARS

We stock largely in all Motor Requisites and Spare Parts
:: :: including large stock of **TYRES.** :: ::
Petrol.   Oil and Grease.   Accumulators Charged.

Official Repairer to the Automobile Club of Great Britain & Ireland.

: REPAIRS EXECUTED BY SKILLED WORKMEN :
ESTIMATES GIVEN for Repairs to any make of Car.

A fine selection of CARS FOR HIRE.

I

The Banbury Cross Garage, an early garage on the
corner of Horse Fair/West Bar.

The father of Hook Norton farmer David Golby worked
for Ewins.

himself in an increasingly competitive
world of local garages. Warwick Road
attracted developments by Young's
Garage, Shire Motor Company and the
Banbury General Motor Company. Each
enterprise was an agent for a different

range of vehicles, yet such was the deter-
mination to succeed that the last of these
firms made much of the slogan for Riley's,
'Cars being for the man who would reach
the height of performance without
plunging into the depths of his pocket.'

Mr Young was equally determined
about sales, and in 1938 he organised a
visit to Fords at Dagenham for prospective
buyers of vehicles available from his
garage.

Another part of the town attractive to
owners of motor-related businesses was
the Middleton Road in Grimsbury. Here
the Lido Service Station, Grimsbury
Motors, City Motors and Bridge Motors
have all, at some stage, contributed to the
street scene, as did a remarkable initiative
by George Mumford. He started by selling
petrol under the cover provided by a
corrugated iron hut, which was in the yard
of the Bell and was financially under-
pinned by Strouds, the nearby butchers.
His brown-smocked appearance, usually
with a cigarette dangling from his mouth,
made him easily recognisable.

In 1954 forecourt improvements by
Youngs on Warwick Road heralded a new
era, one in which a more effective
showroom enabled the garage to display a
wider range of Ford Cars, this gave them
a possible competitive edge over their
local rivals. By 1971 Hartford Motors had
opened up on the Foundry Street corner of
the Warwick Road. It was here that trac-
tors were part of the expanded business.

Apart from one service station and
associated shop selling food, drink and
newspapers, the present day Warwick
Road presents a very different scene. The
huge complex that was Hartford Motors
has now been replaced by the apartments

Chapman's van was fitted
with solid tyres by
Sirmon's of Bridge Street.

Banbury General Motor Company.

Youngs Garage, Warwick Road/Park Road junction (now Bennetts furniture store).

Banbury High Street – County Garages breakdown truck comes to the rescue sometime in the 1950s. The incident attracted much interest from passers-by.

of Clark Court, part of a wave of development of flats and town houses that has rippled across the town.

Banbury Motor Park – a car-retailing concept for the 21st century

Despite the many road improvements and the continued growth of out of town retailing, the sale of motor vehicles still happens at car showrooms dotted irregularly across the town.

Kitewood Estates, in partnership with Axa Real Estate, have devised a scheme known as a dealership cluster. Here car buyers can compare and contrast models and makes at the same destination. The proposed Banbury Motor Park would be at Junction 11 of the M40 motorway, a site notable for its prominence as well as access to the principal gateway to the town.

If this comes about car display and sales will have come a long way from the days of Pytchley Autocars and Sidney Ewins.

Motorway mania

Banbury's development during the past 100 years owes much to the way different forms of transport have evolved. One of the most recent and most important catalysts has been the coming of the M40 motorway in 1992. In effect, it changed the town from a local metropolis and market town into a staging post between London and Birmingham. In the words of William Rayner writing for the

Artist's impression of the motor car dealers' park near the M40.

Independent on Sunday, Banbury had become 'a magnet for distribution and hi-tech firms'. In particular, the town strengthened links with motor sports.

By improving access to this part of Oxfordshire for the population, the M40 resulted in the likes of Debenhams, British Home Stores and Woolworths becoming part of the new Castle Quay shopping centre. The outcome has been a new era of regionalism beyond Banbury.

Another consequence of the motorway has been the targeting of the town and surrounding villages for new housing developments. Some farmers locally have allowed the final phase of rotation to become an estate of houses, which are often snapped up by commuters and retired people from outside the county who have weighed up the economic and social advantages of the good transport links. Further development on the southern edge of Banbury may well be dependent on the construction of a second motorway junction on the Oxford side of the town.

The M40 motorway has hastened economic development in the Banbury area.

SHOPS AND SHOPPING

A town of family traders – an overview

Long before the Castle Shopping Centre took shape in the late 1960s, Banbury's retail reputation had been based on the enterprise of families who often lived above their shops. Among these were many small bakery businesses, each one producing specialities eagerly sought after by people of the town and district.

Mawditts in the Market Place were known for their fruit cakes, Gardiners of Bridge Street made lardy and dough cakes and Browns topped the bill for a Banbury Cake as theirs combined lightness of texture, buttery pastry and a core of rich fruit. In a pre-1939 guidebook to Banbury it is stated that you could buy six of these cakes for 2s 2d (11p) or even 26 for 9s

A typical view along Parsons Street at the start of the 20th century. The Kings Arms (right) closed in 1906.

The Original Cake Shop in Parsons Street where Banbury Cakes had been baked since the 17th century, shown here decorated for the Coronation of Edward VII. Although a listed building, the shop was demolished in 1967 to make way for a new shopping development.

E.W. BROWN.

THE ORIGINAL CAKE SHOP.

LAMB LATE BEESLEY.

THE ORIGINAL CAKE SHOP.

LATE BEESLEY

GOD SAVE THE KING

1638

SALT WAREHOUSE.

HUNTLEY & PALMERS BISCUITS

Interior of Brown's tearoom.

10d (about 49p). Brown's also served lunches and teas in their Parsons Street premises. They reigned virtually unchallenged until the World War Two years when Wincotts of South Bar became a fashionable place to go by day or night.

The original Boots shop in the High Street. Boots Cash Chemists came to the town in 1905.

Of the chain stores, Boots Cash Chemists were established in Banbury High Street in 1905. They were one of the earliest large organisations to enter the town and announced their presence with a huge sign that projected high above the building.

By 1910 W.H. Smith had set up on a corner location formed by the High Street and the Market Approach junction. Like Boots, they had a circulating library, which was popular in the days before fiction could be borrowed from a public library.

Some shop owners in other forms of retailing found ways of cultivating a touch of class in the estimation of customers. Outstanding High Street examples were Judges (ladies' fashions), Gingers (jewellery) and Butlers (groceries). Few people dependent on Banbury's shops are likely to forget the clouds of smoke from ground coffee machines – a most exotic aroma by local standards of the day! Close by Butlers was Colebrook's store that sold a

A Co-op grocery entry in a window display competition. The Banbury and District Industrial Co-operative Society was formed in 1866 and established its first shop in Broad Street in the first decade of the 20th century, and in 1934 it opened the town's first-ever shopping arcade.

The Co-op's shopping arcade as its looks in 2005.

R. Brummitt & Sons

Give you a hearty invitation to look round their premises, which have recently been enlarged and greatly improved.
EVERY DEPARTMENT is now full to overflowing with everything of the latest.

If you require **TRAVELLING REQUISITES** or Leather Goods of any description we have a splendid stock of Dress Baskets, Suit Cases, Gladstone Bags, Hand Bags, Purses, &c.
Commercial and Fancy Stationery at all prices.
FANCY GOODS, TOYS, and GAMES.
ARE YOU AN AMATEUR PHOTOGRAPHER? If so, you will be interested in the up-to-date stock of Photographic Goods we have to show you. Our advice in Photographic Matters is at your disposal.
CREST CHINA, Mounted and Unmounted Views, &c., most suitable as **Souvenirs.**
No one is importuned to Buy.

Make a Note of the Addresses—

57 and 58, Parson's Street, BANBURY.

16

R. Brummitt & Sons had a large department store in Parsons Street selling travel goods, fancy goods, china, toys and games.

J. Harold Judge's ladies' fashion business occupied a central position in the High Street until the 1970s.

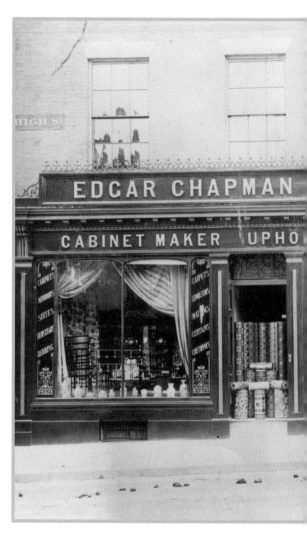

Chapman Bros High Street furnishing store in the early 20th century. Highly regarded for furnishings, they traded in several locations before settling in Bridge Street.

much wider range of fish, fruit and vegetables than is the case of anywhere in the Banbury of 2005.

Since 1913 No. 27 High Street has been home to S.H. Jones, family purveyors of fine wines. Previously there had been a shop on the opposite side and close to the White Lion Hotel, but originally the grandfather of the present owner, Michael Jones, operated from a building on the site of what became Church House.

Among the company treasures are two little booklets with price lists. The earlier one dates to shortly after 1900 and informs us about the prices of the day. Sherries ranged from 18s to 50s (90p–£2.50) per dozen bottles, while 51s (£2.55) secured 12 bottles of excellent champagne.

An equivalent list of the early 1930s

The staff of Francis L. Durran pictured outside their Market Place shop.

St John's Ambulance Cadet Band form part of a Remembrance Day parade marching from Marlborough Road into the High Street. The *c.*17th-century former bakery became S.H. Jones in 1911.

Palmer and Barlow's corn and seed store in the High Street. They also had a canal wharf in Lower Cherwell Street.

reflects an increase in prices but with a fascinating tailpiece on wine management and some useful cocktail recipes. Who could resist trying a Manhattan, a Barnato or indeed Spion Kop?

Parsons Street also had its attractions.

Prominent among these were Dossetts (Butlers great rivals), Brummits toy shop with its amazing selection of model animals and soldiers, Bernard Smith for haberdashery and Pilsworths (clothes) whose advertisements claimed that they catered for distant gentry.

Dossetts traded on the corner of Parsons Street and North Bar from 1887 to 1973. Their shelves were laden with groceries, though on occasions a visit to Butlers was necessary to secure an item not in stock and so avoid disappointing a

A fine view down Parsons Street with Dossett's shop on the left-hand corner.

customer. They also featured wines, spirits and beers. A list for autumn 1967 reveals an astonishing range of bottled alcoholic delights from right across Europe. At 80s 6d (£4.03) and 98 proof, Krepkaya vodka was described as the only genuine Russian vodka produced and bottled in the USSR. A *Banbury Guardian* advertisement for the shop said it all in two slogans, 'We've got it!' and 'Dossetts is Different'.

Just below Dossetts at 41 and 42 Parsons Street were the fresh and fried fish shops of W.A. Truss and Sons. William Arthur Truss acquired these from the Bolton family at the end of World War One, a deal that had ended his desperate search for premises.

Truss brought his fish from a variety of traditional ports like Hull and Lowestoft and supplied customers in and around Banbury, some of whom ran hotels and

William George Dossett, his wife Alice and their daughters. William bought the failed grocery business of Frank Hall in 1887.

boarding houses. As for prices, his boast in the years before 1939 was 'nothing above a shilling'.

Wyncolls had a flourishing fruit, vegetable and flower business at North Bar next to St Mary's Church.

At first Truss delivered by horse and trap, but this was replaced by converted model T Fords, which could accommodate fruit and vegetables as well as fish. In addition to the shops, the Truss family ran stalls in Banbury and Stratford markets. Interestingly, Stratford was by far the busier of the two, necessitating the employment of several assistants.

Last in the line of members of the Truss family to direct the business was John, who retired in 1985 and promptly closed the shop, though the market stall carried on for a while longer. It was also the end of the road for George Buzzard who had been with the family for 50 years.

Close to the Market Place but actually in Bridge Street is Hoods ironmongery shop. Now modernised in layout, the business remains a unique part of the town's fabric. The previous emporium-type building was just the sort of place from which few customers ever emerged

Thai Orchid replaces Wyncolls fruit, vegetables and flowers. A poster advertising a forthcoming Banbury Operatic Society production of 'The Yeomen of the Guard' enjoys a prominent position in St Mary's churchyard.

without having found at least some of the items they were looking for – screws too long, someone would shorten them to your requirements. It was a rabbit warren of a place with numerous rooms of various sizes split up by passageways.

Situated at 35–36 Bridge Street, Hoods was originally owned by S. and E.H. Hood but was bought out by Mr Orchard of Marston House, which was close by on the site of the present Marks and Spencer store. This family business was structured to serve a largely rural Oxfordshire clientele, which back in the 1920s and 1930s was still a world of blacksmiths, wheelwrights and saddlers. There was paraffin in abundance, duplex lamps, grates and ranges for coal fires and tin kettles both new and awaiting repair.

Almost by tradition, the reputation of

the firm was linked to length of service. Typically, Percy Miller gave over 50 years to the business, and at the same time was part of the wider social life of the town as he played in goal for Stones Athletic FC and was a member of the popular Black Diamond dance band.

Trading on or near the corner

Down the years many of the best positions for shop premises have been linked closely to corner sites. In some instances these properties have also been landmark buildings. The Humphris family of builders and undertakers gained a reputation in the late 1920s for a speculative development using art deco design at the point where Bridge Street narrows close to the former Crown Hotel. The *Banbury Guardian* dubbed this 'Humphris' white elephant' as for

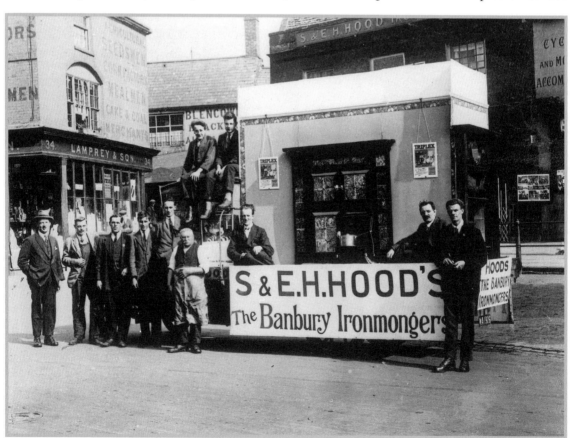

Hoods mobile advertising display unit in the 1930s.

A fine Art deco building, a late 1920s speculative development by the Humphris family.

some while their building remained empty. After a period of several months the potential of the site was recognised by the Shropshire, Staffordshire and Worcestershire Power Company.

The Market Place has some fine corner properties. These include a pre-Civil War building at the junction with Butchers Row. For over 100 years this was occupied and lived in by the Robins family of ironmongers. By the 1920s it was part of a wider scene as Thursday market stalls were huddled in a triangle towards Butchers Row.

At and close to where Butchers Row joins the High Street were some prime positions for shops. Harry Boxold recognised this when he filled his attractive and gabled building with an astonishing range of seeds, fruit and vegetables. This vanished in 1934 when Montague Burton laid the foundation stone for his tailoring

Robins Ironmongery shop occupied a pre-Civil War building at a corner of the Market Place and Butchers Row.

An inter-war view of the lower High Street, full of family businesses but also some chains like Pearks.

A mediaeval tchure at the side of the Vivers building leads from the High Street through to the market.

R.S. Malcolm, family baker and confectioner. The Malcolm family had a bakery in Grimsbury and shops in Grimsbury and in the upper High Street near the Cross. Ray Malcolm holds one of his last trays of Banbury Cakes. The opening of Morrisons superstore had made it increasing difficult to find bakery staff.

business on the site. Once this store was up and running the local manager was not slow to take a whole page of the *Banbury Guardian* in order to announce the bargains and classic items of the day. Favourable prices would have been welcomed by the mass of people in Banbury, for whom the 1930s were economically difficult times. Opportunities to buy at these prices would have overridden any disappointment at the loss of Boxold's building.

Thirty years on, many of the big retail names of the sixties were to be spotted at significant High Street corners. Close to Burtons were the Fifty Shilling Tailors and also Hepworths. Collectively they formed a tailoring cluster of firms specialising in the made-to-measure business.

Another significant and nearby associa-

Happier times, Hugh Scully with Ray Malcolm's Banbury Cakes at an edition of the Antiques Roadshow held in Spiceball Leisure Centre.

Cornhill and part of the north side of the Market Place. Walls and awnings contain lots of information about retailers and stock. A bus is parked in Cornhill and there are seats around a central lamp standard.

tion of buildings was that of the White Lion Hotel, Mawles ironmongery and farm machinery business and, close to these, the Orange Grove greengrocery. In combination, these produced what Oxfordshire planners called 'a lively street façade'. Here, also, was a classic example of an individual who contributed much to retail life in the High Street. Few who were in Banbury some 40 years ago will have forgotten Bill Coles, proprietor of the Orange Grove. His personal attention to the needs of customers was second to none. Bill's command of several Asian languages attracted people from across the spectrum of ethnic minority groups. He also endeared himself to regulars through a ready wit. On one occasion the sale of a bunch of bananas was accompanied by the quip that their excellence owed much to his initiative in picking them that very day before the frost!

The 1922 Shopping Festival

In late May 1922 the tempo of life in the normally quiet market town of Banbury was quickened by the organisation of an exciting and imaginative shopping festival. This event included many activities, but perhaps the most significant was a procession through the principal streets that involved all the leading family shopkeepers.

The festival also marked a change in the outlook of traders who wanted to advance the claims of the town as a marketing and business centre. In a contemporary issue of the *Banbury Guardian* it was stated that 'henceforward the Banbury tradesmen will cease to be mere order takers and will become "demand creators".'

The opening ceremony that launched the Shopping Week was held partly on The Green and partly at the Cross end of

Lady Williams opens the 1922 Shopping Festival.

the High Street. In the wake of speeches, Lady Williams, wife of the area's Member of Parliament, cut a ribbon that released a large balloon and so signalled the start of the festival. The *Guardian* noted that coincidentally 'the bells of the Parish Church rang out a merry peal and the town was en fete.' It is little wonder, therefore, that not only local photographers such as Sansbury and Blinkhorn but also a London Press cameraman covered the occasion.

On Tuesday 30 May the tradesmen of the town took part in the procession that made its way along all the main central streets and then over the bridge and through Grimsbury. Leading fishmongers Turner and Truss entered their light carts, and there were appropriate vehicles on behalf of butchers such as Rathbones and Jelfs. In the section for motor vans Mr

Allen led the way with his brightly coloured Shenington bus that heralded a new generation of public transport capable of bringing in more people from the villages to shop in Banbury.

One of the most effective trade displays was achieved by the County Garage, which occupied premises at the corner of West Bar Street with the Horse Fair. Adorned in yellow and black, this vehicle had a massive motor wheel at the rear and a person in a very large Mr Michelin costume.

Leading the whole process was the symbolic 'lady on a white horse'. She was Mary Anderson, daughter of a local trader, and she wore a most distinctive old English riding costume.

On its way to the High Street the procession came to a halt outside the Town Hall where dancers from Sibford performed a Morris dance.

The County Garage vehicle. In the background are the former Criterion Inn, now Boxholds, the narrow entrance to Church Lane centre and a Banbury Cake advertisement on the building top at the entrance to Butchers Row.

The Lady on the White Horse (Mary Anderson) outside the White Lion in the 1922 Shopping Festival procession.

Maypole dancing accompanies the appearance of cockhorses and hobby horses in 1922.

Two evenings of the Festival Week were taken up with activities entitled Banbury Revels. The scene was the Cow Fair in front of the Town Hall, and the main feature was children dancing around maypoles that had been made in Braggins Gatteridge Street yard. The participating

The Carnival ground at Harriers View during Shopping Week.

schools were St Mary's infants' school, Cherwell Council School for infants, Christ Church (Middleton Road) and Grimsbury Council School. It is certain that people in Banbury had not witnessed an event like this since the early 1600s when Puritan zeal removed our crosses and put an end to activities like Morris and Maypole dancing.

During the shopping event most traders arranged attractive window displays and some took part in a competition. Wherever there was a red disc in the window members of the public had to identify an item that was not normally sold by the participating traders. This inspired the *Banbury Guardian* cartoonist G.D. Coles, who depicted a gentleman over indulging himself in spotting activities. When prizes were awarded for the best-dressed window a judge from Aldershot declared that Banbury's stan-

Banbury and District Chamber of Trade, organisers of the Festival.

dards were akin to those of some West End stores.

Seasonal shopping attractions

Christmases past have often been made a bit special by the seasonal arrangements of family-run businesses in Banbury. Many 1920s shoppers intent on goodies would have made their way to Browns famous cake shop in Parsons Street. Apart from attractively wrapped Banbury Cakes there was the added bonus of 'Ride-a-Cockhorse' crackers.

In 1922 H. Gibbs, also of Parsons Street, benefited from a share of game on the Heythrop Estate near Chipping Norton. Turners of Broad Street included prize-winning fowl in their renowned display – two of the geese had caught the eye of judges at the annual Christmas Fat Stock Show.

Opportunities for Christmas shopping in general were sometimes proclaimed through the advertising enterprise of the Banbury Chamber of Trade. In 1920 the final *Banbury Guardian* issue of the year included a box in which was written 'every conceivable want for the Christmas season will be shown in profusion at prices that will stand the keenest competition'. The Chamber added that shops would be open all day on 19 December, and this in a town that adhered strictly to the tradition of half-day closing.

Many individual retailers added their own inimitable styles of advertising. In 1925 Robins the Market Place ironmongers featured their Aladdin Lamps, 'the

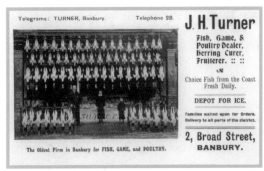

Turner's display of Christmas fowl at their shop in Broad Street.

Fox's corner, an impressive feature of Bridge Street. The entrance to the old bus station can be seen on the extreme left.

empire's most wonderful form of illumination'. A single lamp's 80-candle power cost one old penny for an 8-hour burn time.

Some shop owners even resorted to verse. Chards of Parson's Street, who traded as Ye Olde Bacy Shoppe at that time, devised the following lines:

'There is an old shop called Chard's
Sells 'Twist' by yards upon yards
And this is no jest, it's the best
Place in the town for cigars.'

New Year bargains of the 1920s made a trip to Banbury town centre worthwhile. Fox's, the Grimsbury and Parsons Street chemist, had a Kodak camera on offer for 10s 6d (just over 52p). Arkell Bros, outfitters at 61 High Street, announced in the *Banbury Guardian* 'we sort over and clear

up the merchandise which at this time… resembles nothing so much as a Dog's Breakfast or the remains of the annual turkey.'

In the early 1930s getting to the sales was partly in the hands of the Birmingham and Midland Red Bus Company, which was not always an enjoyable experience. A.H.C. Weston, writing in the *Guardian* letters column, drew attention to the dependence of local shops on people from the villages.

His seemingly justifiable complaint was that passengers had no official shelter in which to await return services. He wrote that many times he had heard the comment 'good job Woolworth's have come, it will be somewhere warm to wait for the bus'.

Christmas lights in the High Street in 1956.

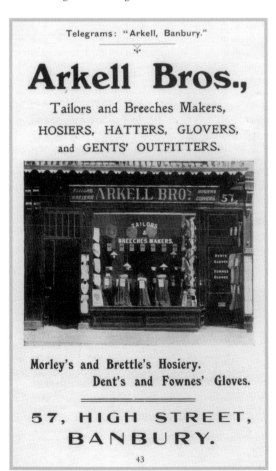

The changing retail scene of today

The present day town has a dwindling number of family businesses. Gone are the bakers and fishmongers and most of the butchers, grocers and greengrocers. In December 2003 this trend was accentuated by the closure of Ekins in Church Lane after some 65 years of trading. This business grew out of a firm of Northampton bespoke shoemakers and turned into a pattern of sales embracing clothing, curtain materials, household linens and knitting wools. In the 1950s and 1960s especially, stock was very much dominated by the needs of the working man. Farmers who had come into Banbury for the livestock market were especially important customers. They often departed Ekins clutching their Derby tweeds or Bedford cords.

Arkell Bros – one of the many bespoke tailors in Banbury before World War One.

Wincott's Café with
William Stroud
(butcher) above.

Bridge Street in the 1980s, shortly after road alterations left Hammonds Electrical and Masons family butchers somewhat isolated.

The centre part of the High Street in 2002. The tallest building in this part of the High Street had been Boots in 1905. Note the number of agents' boards – an impact of Castle Quay development.

Other specialist clothing needs targeted by Ekins were those of schools and scouts, but there were also lucrative contracts for work clothes with firms such as R.O. Wright (structural engineers), the Northern Aluminium Company and Export Packing. In the early 60s, when Alfred Bird's convenience foods factory was under construction, major contractors Matthew Hall generated an 'insatiable hunger for wellies'. Boots could only be worn by one person and so there was a constant need to replace the discarded ones, which were then incinerated.

By the time the Castle Quay Shopping Centre opened in 2000 Ekins had closed its shoe department with its Doc Marten boots and the farmers' macs past history. The axis of retailing in Banbury had moved eastwards. White Lion Walk and Church Lane suffered the effect of a

Ekins of Church Lane, the retirement of David Hitchcock caused the closure of the business.

decline in passing trade. 'For sale' boards became a familiar sight in the High Street where some properties remain slow to let.

Currently the High Street is undergoing a bit of a renaissance but this is based more on service activities such as hairdressing than on traditional retailing.

Promotional spot of the original Castle Shopping Centre.

However, the well-known name of Moss Bros. has come to fill the old Burton's store and close by is a Chelsea firm specialising in quality teas and coffees. It remains to be seen if some family enterprises in Calthorpe Street and the Cross end of the High Street can draw benefit from an increased number of visitors attracted by the Lady on the White Horse statue.

Castle Quay's development has taken Banbury into an age of blue chip companies when it is a position within a national shopping league table that really matters. The M40 has placed the town in the reach of a shopping catchment of some 100,000 people. Firms like Debenhams, British Home Stores, Gap and Next have responded to the associated opportunities. However, retail euphoria was really complete for some when the Ann Summers chain decided that Banbury was indeed not a commercial venture too far!

Family businesses can and do survive and are to be found in the area around the

Bridge Street in 2004, a much changed scene. The entrance to the new bus station is centre next to the board just past the jutting out arcaded building.

Cross, in Parsons Street and off the High Street. Hoods alone have a presence in the original Castle Shopping Centre. Typical

Ventilation installation in the Castle Quay Centre calls for the tallest crane seen in Banbury.

of the long-established businesses still trading is Blinkhorns.

Blinkhorns Photographic

Since 1880, Blinkhorns has been one of Banbury's outstanding family businesses. Its founder was Thomas Jeffer Hammond Blinkhorn. He set up his studio in South Bar. This was a large, wooden barn-like structure but with a substantial skylight so that those who posed, usually in their best clothes, would only have to keep still for a brief moment. Daylight was vital to his work because he exposed his glass plates in the yard close to the studio.

In common with many other business people of the day, Thomas frequently set off in his pony and trap to visit his customers in their own homes. Many of his clients lived in villages and would have found it difficult to get to the South Bar

Bridge Street – Castle Quay viewed from Malthouse Walk.

studio. Early in the 20th century Thomas diversified his activities by opening a Picture House in Banbury Market Place. Here silent films were shown and travelling shows presented. Like the photography, the operation of the cinema was a family affair with daughter-in-law Dorothy running the box office.

Next in line to carry on the business was son Norman. He also concerned himself greatly with wider community matters – the Borough Council as an elected representative, Banbury Rotary Club and the Scout Movement. In 1938 he achieved the ultimate accolade within his profession by becoming president of the

Family group in 1907 of Thomas (founder of the business), Bernard, Edith (née Aspell) and Norman (who later took over the business).

Blinkhorns in 1932 showing fire damage to the photographic studio.

Institute of Photography. This must have been some compensation for the dreadful fire of 1932 that destroyed his father's wooden studio and with it a substantial number of glass plates.

On resumption of business in a new studio, Norman took over from his father and developed an associated shop. This provided the opportunity to begin 16mm film making and to sell cameras and photographic equipment. He also operated a mobile film unit, which he deployed widely and quite often at Banbury County School.

Between 1939 and 1945 Blinkhorns were deeply involved in the war effort. Norman helped to run the Air Training Corps and did much photography of service personnel and of secret items as directed by the War Office.

In 1950 Martin Blinkhorn took the helm and for some 50 years directed and developed the photographic business and expanded into sound systems in a way that would surely have pleased his father and grandfather. Like Norman, he was very community minded and played a huge part in local theatre with companies like the Old Banburians and Banbury Cross Players.

Now Martin's son Thomas Jeffer is pursuing a successful route down the high-tech electronic road. He has inherited a business that a past advertisement in a Banbury Round Table booklet proclaimed was all about 'a flash with no bang'. Whether by daylight or flash, four generations of Blinkhorns have a reputation for getting you or your event on camera, as many of the illustrations in this book testify.

The new shop fascia designed by Randolph Harper in 1938, which was built over the top of the 1883 old shop front.

Blinkhorns current shop front in 2004.

IT'S OFF TO WORK WE GO

In 1905 the manufacturing scene in Banbury and district was still very much dominated by businesses that had grown up with the market town during the Victorian era or even earlier in the case of brewing, plush and girth weaving. In the second half of the 19th century a consoli- dated area of industrial development grew up in the Cherwell area near the canal, especially those industries connected with engineering. Samuelson's Agricultural Implements and Engineering Works, Barrows Engineering and Henry Stone's box works were major employers estab-

Cherwell industrial area before the Hunt Edmunds chimney came down in 1972.

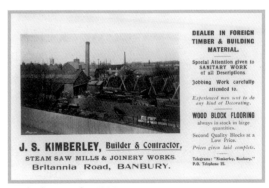

Kimberley's yard *c*.1905.

Cobbs tweed mill had been in Spiceball Park.

Barrows engineering machinery found on a farm near Lockington, Victoria, Australia.

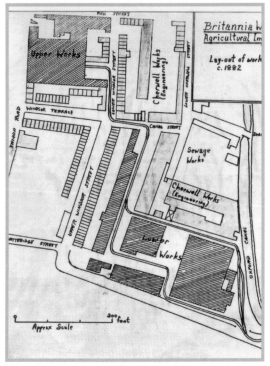

Samuelsons men. The tramway can be seen bottom left.

lished in this area. Elsewhere Lucas and Company (underclothing), Banbury Tweed Factory, Braggins (gate and gate hinges) and Lampreys continued to achieve considerable success.

Samuelson's Britannia Works
By the time Bernhard Samuelson died in 1905 his Britannia Works had ceased to enjoy its period of dominance of the world markets. Competitors in agricultural

Plan of the Britannia Works. The works remained the same until a disastrous fire just before World War One.

Market Place, and William Linnell Lamprey (his son) launched the company into a late Victorian expansionist era by exploring new channels of trade. One of these was the evolution of a brick, tile and pottery works near Duke Street in Grimsbury. In 1905 they topped the million mark for bricks produced.

Lamprey's shop at the eastern end of the Market Place.

This side of company affairs attracted the attention of *The Gentlemen's Journal*. In their edition of 27 June 1908 much is made of Lamprey's ability to exploit a huge outcrop of Oxford blue clay. These works were closed in the early 20th century but the abandoned pit provided children with an informal adventure playground for some years to follow.

The Lampreys were also busy on the canalside. Here at Wharf Mill close to Lower Cherwell Street and Bridge Wharf there were huge lime kilns using raw materials worked at Shipton-on-Cherwell and brought by barge to Banbury.

In 1901 a new name became associated with the Lampreys when William married May Jane Bradshaw. Her father was miller and baker at Wykham Mill, halfway between Banbury and Bloxham. This was a water mill fed by a watercourse linked to the Sor Brook.

Between 1919 and 1939 the key figure

implement manufacture arose in Britain and America, but the real blow was a serious fire in 1912 that destroyed part of the lower works coupled with the impact of World War One that led to labour shortages and severance of markets. Despite a brief and considerable success with the sales of milling machinery, the company never recovered. The ultimate cause was the early 30s depression, which made closure inevitable.

Lamprey's and the Wykham Mill connection

Lamprey's trade, like Samuelson's, was initially based on the agricultural needs of the area. They were undoubtedly best known for their major corn merchanting business. However, John Lamprey, who lived above his shop on the fringe of the within the company was Nelson Bradshaw. He steered the business through the depression years of the 1920s but inevitably had to close a wharf and mill in Banbury to ensure Wykham's viability. With the drive to get most from the land during World War Two came the opportunity to diversify into chemical sprays.

The 1950s and 1960s saw the Wykham Mill business grow, and the company took over the Cherwell-side mill of Edmunds and Kench. These were the decades of Roger Bradshaw's influence.

By 1980 computerisation had taken Lampreys into a new world, but perhaps the most nostalgic happening was reserved for the restoration of the mill wheel at Wykham by Aston Martin Lagonda, who at the time produced their high-quality cars on the site. To see the newly restored

wheel revolving was a fine reminder of the contribution made to local industry that can be attributed to the Lampreys and later to their partnership with the Bradshaws.

Hunt Edmunds

By the early part of the 20th century the brewing trade had come to be dominated by Hunt Edmunds with their huge complex between Bridge and George Streets.

The secrets of their success came to be revealed in a pamphlet issued by the firm to mark its involvement in the Banbury Industrial Exhibition of 1951. In this Hunt Edmunds made a very telling statement: the company 'has a tall chimney and a big heart'. The story behind the second of these assets can be told by reference to its workforce and the range of products.

A 1960s view of Hunt Edmunds from Cherwell Street.

Hunt Edmunds workforce, *c.*1911.

Les Sims of Kings Sutton records bottled beer stored at Hunt Edmunds.

Length of service and adaptability appear to have been important factors. Typical was Alf Hone who worked as a young lad in the bottle room, then with Hunt Edmunds' dray horses and finally on the delivery lorries.

The malthouse was another part of the brewery that benefited from long association. Reg Adams was foreman malster for 48 years and made himself responsible for the early stages of the beer-making process.

On the products side of the business trade price lists are an invaluable source of information. In its brochure for Christmas 1953 the company spoke of its own 'high quality' beers – Banbury Cross Ale, Banbury Brown Ale and Banbury Best Bitter. There were also firsts in the beer lines, as in 1964 when a new pale ale was brought out just before Whitsun. Discerning drinkers detected a richer taste and fuller body.

There is every reason to understand why Doug Golby wrote in a *Banbury Guardian* article 'brewing today stands proud as the lone survivor of the old market-town skills' – a far cry from the picture back in 1905. In 1967 the Hunt Edmunds' properties were sold, divided between Mitchell and Butler and Bass Charrington. Sadly Doug Golby's observations ceased to be relevant when the tall chimney of the 1951 statement came crashing to the ground some 20 years later in 1974. In 2005, apart from archival material, the only tangible memory of Hunt Edmunds are examples of the distinctive pub plaque fixed to former tied houses that can still be spotted on the walls of the Blarney Stone in Cherwell Street and the Wheatsheaf in George Street, as well as some of the more outlying inns like the Warwick Road premises of the Duke of Wellington.

Henry Stone and Son

In 1928 Henry Stone and Son Ltd issued a brochure commemorating 60 years of manufacture. Its beautiful illustrations underlined the importance of high-grade colour printing and fine art reproduction.

In the early 1870s Henry Stone, a High Street stationer, invented a new type of box file that looked like a book. Its manufacture was the basis of the company's

Stones Printing and Box Factory.

later furniture business. Expansion was very much linked to Lewis Wycherley Stone, the founder's son. Under his direction the furniture and printing aspects grew substantially, and by 1915 the photo-engraving and colour printing work had expanded and moved to Swan Close.

All the buildings have now disappeared and become part of Banbury's history. The printing works was on land that is now part of Morrisons superstore, and the furniture factory has been replaced by apartments, which being situated on a brownfield site was an obvious attraction for developers.

Spencer House

During the late 1920s Dorothea Allen set up a very different kind of business on the western edge of the Cherwell area when

Spencer Corsets had a reputation for ensuring a good fit.

she established a factory to manufacture underwear in Spencer House. This enterprise was a departure for Banbury and diversified the working environment of Britannia Road, which was already home to Stone's box factory and Kimberley's builders yard.

By the end of the 1930s the Spencer factory was capable of sustaining a large

The canteen at Spencer's.

A busy production room
at Spencers in the 1930s.

workforce. Along with the Northern Aluminium Company in the Southam Road, the firm was a vital part of Banbury's industrial renaissance. The building occupied by this underwear firm became a substantial symbol of the town's recovery after the closure of the Britannia Works at the end of the 1920s had plunged Banbury into a run of depression years.

From then until Spencers closed in 1989 the firm was rarely out of the local news. Increasingly, economic success was shown as dependent on relocation to an industrial estate on the edge of Banbury. A 1980s article by Keith Wood, senior reporter for the *Guardian*, carried the banner headline 'Corset Company bursting at the seams'.

Early in 2005 Spencer House was demolished amid much controversy.

Those in favour of retention were conscious of the amount of local interest generated by a building that had been designed by Wallis Gilbert and Partners of London in the 1920s art deco style. English Heritage may have been correct in their assessment of this extension to the former Lucas factory as no more than humble but the art deco entrance hall was pleasing to the eye and Spencers very much part of the Britannia Road urban scene. In the word of the *Banbury Guardian* for 10 February, 'this drama… can be seen as part of a wider movement towards re-imaging this part of Banbury. Apartments and not factories are coming to dominate the streetscape.'

The Northern Aluminium Company

In 1951 George Braggins, president of the Chamber of Commerce, penned a brief

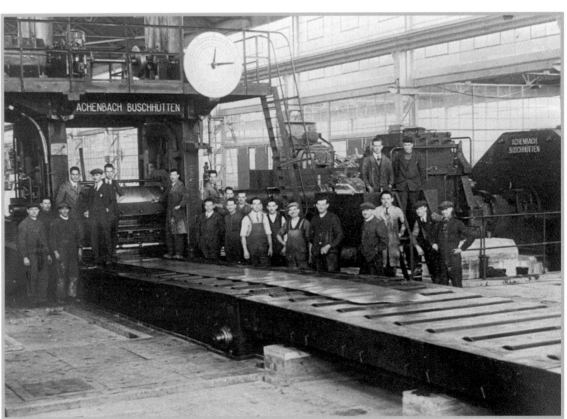

Northern Aluminium Company (Alcan) rolling mill.

but important message for visitors to Banbury's industrial exhibition. 'Banbury? Oh yes that's where the cakes come from. Or, I know "Ride a Cockhorse, etc" is the usual answer. Our job today… is to endeavour to bring Banbury to the notice of the world as a growing industrial centre.' That he was able to say this at all owes much to the establishment and growth of the Northern Aluminium Company in the 1930s.

In contrast with Spencers, the Northern Aluminium Company began life on the edge of the town. It set up its works on the Southam Road and early in the 1930s was employing some 1,800 men, including migrants from Lancashire and Yorkshire mill towns.

The improvement in the local job scene happened despite unrest at the factory that culminated in one of the biggest mass meetings ever to be held in the Market Place – 1,600 people gathered here on a Sunday evening in 1935. The workforce was seeking a pay rise and also the right to set up their own branch of the Transport and General Workers Union. The strike was a brief one, and it was only in the slightly longer term that wage packets reflected a 1d an hour increase and employees were able to smoke (another grievance was the no smoking policy) if they so wished.

Job losses at the Britannia Works were also balanced by the enterprise of farmer Henry Owen Bennett who set up a manufactory for ladies knitwear in St John's Road and by the establishment of Switchgear and Equipment whose business grew out of the need for electrification in the Banbury area.

On the move – Alfred Bird and Sons

In the mid-1960s industrialisation was given a new direction by the arrival of Alfred Bird (General Foods Ltd), famous for its celebrated custard powder and later Angel Delight. The firm moved from Deritend, Birmingham, to a 31-acre site, where an important feature is the Max-

Bird's Factory (General Foods) in September 1965. Nearby Ruscote Avenue looks like a country lane.

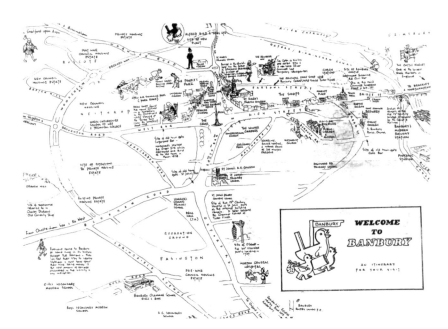

Sketch map of Banbury drawn by Frank Toole in 1966 and designed to help Bird's workers find their way around as they moved from Deritend in Birmingham.

well House coffee-making plant that is now a landmark on the Banbury skyline.

At a time when industry was being directed to areas in need of redevelopment in the North East, North West and South Wales, Birds were allowed to relocate to Banbury because the land they occupied already had a development certificate (a windfall site liberated by British Nylon Spinners decision to go elsewhere). Part of this land also attracted the Spares Division of Automotive Products Ltd. The two new companies formed the basis of the Beaumont Industrial Estate.

The M40 effect

The arrival of the M40 motorway in 1991 quickened the pace of economic development in the Banbury area. A central location nationally combined with effective transport links favoured the growth of distribution businesses such as Booker Foods, financial service companies like Alex Lawrie Factors and the growth of rally driving enterprises and the luxury end of car manufacturing. Subaru has prospered and until recently when a

The Banbury Business Park at Adderbury.

Banbury's rallying connection – Subaru vehicles leave Prodrive.

takeover by Ford moved them down the road to Gaydon, Aston Martin Lagonda could be found at Wykham Mill on the western outskirts of the town.

Printing

An emergent industrial activity over a much longer period of time has been

A scene of devastation at Cheneys. The fire of 1923 was a severe blow, not least because the firm could no longer produce its popular Railway Guide.

printing. Despite its small size in earlier centuries, Banbury supported two firms, Cheneys and Rushers. The former survived until comparatively recent times and after generations in a central location ended its days on the Beaumont Industrial Estate. No one who has seen Cheneys race cards for steeple chasing, railway guides and notices of all description can doubt the importance of the company in the industrial annals of North Oxfordshire.

2005 – the multi-nationals

Changes of ownership and an inevitable movement towards multi-national control have come to dominate the 21st-century industrial scene in Banbury. Aluminium research activity has been discontinued and transferred from the Southam Road site to Kingston, Ontario and Switzerland, which are nearer to the parent organisations. Opposite to the former laboratories, the aluminium works buildings remain

Some of Cheney's men.

active but the signboard says Alcoa not Alcan (Northern Aluminium Company).

Soon after arrival in Banbury, Alfred Bird's custard factory became General Foods and today the name Kraft Foods hints at its worldwide significance. The administrative nerve centre is now in Cheltenham and the famous custard powder has found a new home with Premier Foods. Fortunately, the famous chicks still adorn the main gate, a reminder of that remarkable move from Deritend to Banbury in the mid-60s.

Thatching of the Three Pigeons – an old craft
survives into modern times.

THE CLASS OF...

Profiling the education scene

Prior to the creation of a National Board of Education in 1899, management of elementary schools was in the hands of locally-elected school boards. Most were allied to either the National Schools (Church of England) or the British Schools (Non-Conformist). At the close of the 19th-century, education was in deep crisis in Banbury. The British Schools located in Crouch Street had been central to provision in the town, but by 1899 it was clear that they could not be reconstructed to meet the target places set by the newly formed Board of Education. Inevitably, closure followed in January the following year.

Cherwell Infants School class III. Frederick Owen Bailey, born 29 July 1901, is on the extreme left, back row.

Managers of other schools in Banbury then met the Town Council and the outcome was promises of additional places at St John's Roman Catholic Schools, St Mary's National Schools, Christchurch National Schools, the Dashwood Road Wesleyan Schools and Cherwell British Schools. These assurances satisfied the Board and so the voluntary system in Banbury was saved.

An education act of 1902 empowered County, Borough and Urban Councils to control elementary, secondary and technical education. Within three years the Borough Council had control of elementary education and became responsible for the Dashwood Road Schools, which had a mixed and infants department until 1932 when the younger children moved to the Cherwell School in Britannia Road (the Samuelson School).

The plaque from former Britannia Road School.

In Grimsbury the existing Wesleyan School moved into a new building on the Middleton Road in 1910 and was the start of the area's council schools.

During the inter-war years under the terms of the Hadow Report and a further act of 1936 the school leaving age should have been raised and separate junior and senior schools established. However, financial difficulties in the 1930s and the outbreak of war in 1939 delayed these changes. A new council school was planned for the Harriers Ground but this did not come about until 1948.

Banbury Municipal School Football Team 1911–12. Seated right end of row is Bernard Blinkhorn and Bill Mardon (teacher) is in the centre. Norman Scroxton, later head of Grimsbury County School, is seated on Mr Mardon's right.

One of the early influential figures in local education was the industrial entrepreneur and MP Bernhard Samuelson. Apart from covering the cost of constructing the Cherwell School, he developed a new and larger Mechanics Institute in Marlborough Road to replace outgrown premises in Church Passage. His building had upper floor space for the Banbury School of Science and Art. As this matured it turned into the Municipal School leased by the Trustees to the County Council in 1923. Seven years later overcrowding and inadequate equipment

This building housed the Banbury Municipal School (now Banbury Library).

A college class over the library at Marlborough Road.

prompted a search for a new location. The outcome was land at Easington for a school with an extensive playing field. Mr Luscombe, who had been headmaster since 1906, launched the school on its new site, but in January 1935 Mr Rose succeeded him. The School of Art and evening classes remained at Marlborough Road until their reorganisation by the Banbury Technical Institute and adoption within the North Oxfordshire Technical College and School of Art. Founders of the art education movement such as the Beales would be well satisfied at today's arrangements that embrace graphics and fashion as well as art and range from leisure classes to degree courses in conjunction with Leicester De Montfort University.

Some Primary experiences

Several primary schools in Banbury have had great cause for celebration in recent years. Two of these are Dashwood Road and St Mary's School.

Dashwood Road was 100 years old in 2002. Its opening owed much to initiatives by the Wesleyan Methodists who created it as a non-denominational school. Three years later Banbury Borough Council took it over after acquiring Local Educational Authority status under an Education Act in 1902.

The period from 1932 to 1952 was an interesting one in the life of this former Wesleyan school. Education had been extended to the age of 14 and so school years were a formative influence, especially for a lady called June Kent who became a teacher in the mid-1940s under the headship of the recently arrived John Proctor. The school seemed rather drab with its institutional brown and green paint, but a routine was well established. June collected money for milk and dinners, gave free cod liver oil to those with entitlement, loaned or issued plimsolls and made arrangements for visits by the school nurse and mobile dentist.

In the 1940s the limitations due to inadequate buildings were clear to see. Drill (PE) happened in the playground if dry or in the aisles between desks when inclement conditions prevailed.

Handicraft tuition meant walks to off-site locations. In the case of boys, woodwork involved getting to a building in Calthorpe Street.

During the years John Proctor was in charge the school changed considerably. Gone was the image of bleak classrooms with high windows and a tortoise stove. By 1968 Dashwood Road had a library and swimming pool and there were annual visits to parts of Europe. Since then successive heads have guided pupils from an increasingly multicultural catchment area and taken on board the curriculum changes common to all primary schools.

The present St Mary's C of E Primary School in the Southam Road was created out of an amalgamation of the Bluecoat Charity School (formerly in the Market Place) with a newly formed National School in 1817.

Day-to-day life within the school can be traced through entries in consecutive logbooks. These highlight special occasions such as May Day. On 1 May 1906 the comment appears 'numbers very poor, many of the children having gone out with garlands'. This was despite a then recent increase in the size of the school because of the admission of extra pupils following the closure of the British Schools in

Crouch Street in 1900. Structural alterations to the Southam Road buildings at about the same time had made possible separate provision for boys, girls and infants.

The man whose headship took in the early 20th century was a Mr G. Kent. He was given the nickname of Tucky and clearly had a reputation for discipline. Not for nothing was he the subject of an amusing rhyme:

'Mr Kent is a very good man
He goes to church on Sunday.
He asks the Lord to give him strength
To wallop his kids on Monday.'

Entries in logbooks continued right up until the mid-1950s. Those for the war year 1940 are especially interesting because of the school's involvement with Banbury's role as a safe haven for evacuees, especially those from London. By 23 June of that year 64 evacuees had been registered. Further increases brought the school roll to 225 by September. St Mary's also gained teachers from London. A Miss Warn from West Ham came as a Physical Training specialist.

After the war local pupils of the school achieved considerable success in securing

places at what had become known by then as Banbury Grammar School.

More recently St Mary's pupils have become increasingly involved in community activities. During the recent visit of Princess Anne in May to unveil the statue of the Lady on the White Horse, the children performed appropriate dances nearby in the Horse Fair. Tercentenary status in 2005 was suitably celebrated with a series of events involving the school, church and town.

By contrast with the great age of St Mary's and Dashwood Road, Harriers Ground Primary School was a post-war creation. It was built on part of the former

1962 Prize Giving at St Mary's School.

Easington Farm and was opened on 21 July 1949 by the Mayor of Banbury, Mrs Mary Cheney. Remarkably, this was the first primary school to be opened in the town since 1912. Prompting development of a new school was the national phenomenon of a baby boom and the local impact of companies like the Northern Aluminium Company fuelling the housing market. The second influence may well have inspired the County Education Committee to consider using aluminium for the construction of the school buildings. Hesitation was because of concerns about durability. Hermione Hitchens, education chairman, is quoted as saying 'I have asked that question myself and I was told to look at the statute of Eros in Piccadilly that has been there for 69 years'. The school she helped to open was made of brick! More importantly, Harriers was a step on the way to securing a primary and secondary school within easy reach of every neighbourhood in Banbury.

The situation in Grimsbury

The earliest primary school in Grimsbury was at Christ Church National School in the Middleton Road and dated from 1862. In 1921 this became St Leonard's Grimsbury Church of England School, adjacent to the church, which had been

Grimsbury County School pupils assembled for the Annual prize giving in November 1957. At the top table, top to bottom: the Mayor, Councillor M. Spokes, Lady Saye and Sele, Lord Saye and Sele (father of present Lord), Mr V.E.T. Jones (chairman of Governors), headmaster Norman Scroxton. In his address, Lord Saye and Sele told the children 'Do to others as you would like them to do to you. You must not expect everything to go the way you like because it won't.'

consecrated a Chapel-of-Ease and daughter institution of Christ Church, South Banbury, in 1891. By 1950 two names that stood out on the staff list were Miss Watts and Mr Spencer. The latter used to organise a very popular May Festival.

Grimsbury Council School was established in School View in 1909. Its main catchment was the Merton Street and Causeway area and, as many of the people in these streets were chapel folk, there was a strong link with Methodism. At the outset there was education for children between the ages of three and 14 but under the 1944 Education Act it became an 11 to 14 establishment. When Harry Judge developed a federation of halls for Banbury School, the School View building briefly became Grimsbury Hall.

Primary age children moved into new premises in East Street in 1957. By the time its first head Brenda Lukasinska retired in 1978 it had become multicul-

tural, and school celebrations had widened to include a feast for the end of Ramadan with appropriate games and food. Pupils also revived the custom of dancing round a maypole and crowning May Kings and Queens, much as was practised by the children of the first school.

Banbury County School

A red-letter day in Banbury's educational history was 23 May 1930 when the Right Hon Sir Charles Trevelyan, Bart, MP opened the new County School. Hinkins and Frewin of Oxford constructed the two-storey brick building in Ruskin Road known as Banbury County School. Completed at a cost of £30,000, it had provision for 360 pupils, 90 more than the Marlborough Road roll call of 270, which had resulted in overcrowding.

A place at the County School, like most grammar schools of the day, was dependent on a fee paid by the child's parents or guardians. It was quite a break-

Some of the staff and pupils of Banbury County School in 1937 after the move to Ruskin Road.

She Stoops to Conquer 1936. Far left, Enid Lickorish (Beere), centre (Sir) Jack Johnson, third from right Ken Mills (now Ken Wynne Royal Shakespeare Co and TV actor).

The Ladies Cricket Team, Banbury County School, in 1936. Front, left to right: Jean Hutchinson, Enid Lickorish (Beere), Olive Cadd, –?–, –?–,. Back: Nan Webber, Jean Perfitt, Vera Hunnysett, Mary Lamb, Freda Mallett, Sue Francis.

through when in the 1930s trustees of the Blue Coat Charity School (St Mary's) decided to finance two exhibitions for local pupils accepted by Banbury County School. Each was worth at least £11, and the offer was open to all young people of Banbury Borough who had attended an elementary school for at least two years and not yet reached their 13th birthday. The first awards went to pupils of

Grimsbury County School – Ismay Ellen Jarvis from Centre Street and Sylvia Dean who lived on Middleton Road. Further allowances of money were paid for school uniforms and in Ismay's case a bicycle to get her to Ruskin Road. When it became clear that the pupils showed promise academically the awards were extended until they were 18. Six years later another milestone was reached at the County School when Enid Beere became the first girl exhibitioner to attend university – Royal Holloway College, London, where she read French and Latin.

In early December 1997 Hugh Williams, now living in Newport, Gwent, wrote to the *Banbury Guardian* with his memories of Banbury County School during the war years 1939–41. His house group was Wykeham, which gave rise to shouts of 'Wack-em' when their rugby team took to the field. The other houses were called Hugh, Stanbridge and Compton. The names had historical significance: St Hugh was a Bishop of Lincoln and thus Lord of the Manor of Banbury; John Stanbridge was the early 16th-century Master of the Hospital of St John; William of Wykeham was a mediaeval owner of Broughton Castle and Sir William Compton, at only 17 years of age, was the royalist commander of Banbury Castle during the Civil War.

It was during Hugh Williams's time at the school that the County School incorporated the evacuated Fulham Girls and Bow Central Schools. In February 1940 a serious fire considerably reduced teaching space and so pupils were housed in a variety of town establishments including the Town Hall and nearby St Hugh's Church.

In 1944 an important expansion of the school curriculum was achieved by the incorporation of a Technical Department for boys of 12 and 13. Charles Emmott was put in charge and it was under his direction that four years later girls were

North Oxfordshire Technical School *c.*1950, Woodgreen. Seated centre Mr Charles Emmett, on his right, Eddie Merryfield (deputy head) and Jack Davies (business studies), on his left, Margaret Stanley (senior mistress) and June Kent (English, art).

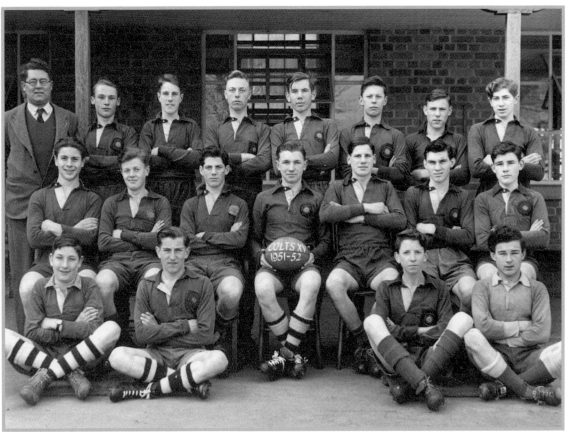

Banbury Grammar School Colts Rugby XV, 1951–52.

A very formal 1930s art room.

admitted to the department and pupils moved to Woodgreen in the Broughton Road, the former home of the Gilletts, the renowned local banking family.

A campus emerges

The Education Act of 1944 led to a complete reorganisation of the provision of 11+ education, dividing children into Grammar and Secondary Modern Schools according to academic ability as registered in special exams sat at the age of 11. Existing schools could not cope with the new demands, and by the 1950s it was clear that additional land close to Ruskin Road was going to become an educational campus. Easington Modern School for Boys opened in 1952 when pupils were accepted from Dashwood Road and St Mary's Schools. In its issue for 21 March 1952 the *Oxford Mail* highlighted the fact that the boys' school had been built almost entirely from aluminium supplied

Derek Fairbairn with his under-14 side at Easington Boys School.

by the locally-based Northern Aluminium Company.

In the 1960s relations between staff and pupils were formal but this did not stop the spread of nicknames for teachers. The headmaster was generally known as 'Bookie' Page. Then there was 'Digger' Gardner who taught English and 'Costa' Coles the Rural Science teacher.

Well-remembered pupils included David Excell who became landlord of the Buck and Bell in North Bar. Other

By the 1990s the same room had become the European Business Centre of Banbury School.

Wykham Hall (formerly Easington Boys School), the long aluminium building, shortly before demolition.

contemporaries were, Ian Durham who combined stock car racing with management of 'Car Bodies' and speedway rider Mick Bell who rode for Oxford as well as Reading and Leicester and later saw management experience at Swindon and Coventry.

Five years later Easington School for Girls was established directly opposite to the boys' building. Apart from the usual subjects within a secondary modern, there was an enterprising domestic science programme as well as secretarial courses at the girls' school.

1967 was another milestone year in the history of education on the Easington Campus. Under the recently appointed head of Banbury Grammar School (the Old County School) a comprehensive was formed catering for the educational needs of over 2,000 students and a federation of halls created with a separate Upper School. The former Grammar School

became known as Stanbridge, Easington Boys was named Wykham, Easington Girls acquired the title of Broughton and, more distantly, Grimsbury Council School, which also provided secondary education, turned into Grimsbury Hall. All these developments inspired the editor of the *Banburian* magazine to comment that 'members of staff whiz round the campus and down to Grimsbury like balls on a pin-table'.

Many former pupils remember Norman Scroxton, who looked after Grimsbury County School in School View, with affection. Undoubtedly, he owed his reputation to the way he identified with pupils through an informal approach, especially in the playground. During the summer term Norman's set of stumps was the basis of impromptu cricket, and at all seasons he was intensely proud of the official school sport teams.

In 1962 a Roman Catholic Secondary

Pupils at Wykham Hall of Banbury School in 1977. Back row, left to right: Jonathan Coles, Jacqueline Jones, Ian Workman, Caroline Little (Winn), Brian Clewley, Lorraine Beckham, Mark Jarvis, Diane Booker, Alan Parr. Second row: Sheena Appleton, Graham Curtis, Kim Jones, David Harvey, Joanne Gow, Terry Falkner, Denise Oliver, Robert Southwell. Front row: Kenneth Keates, Jonathan –?–, Peter Denscombe, Adrian Heritage, Anthony Maycock, Alan Harris, Martin Selby.

School, the Blessed George Napier, opened its doors to an initial intake of 171 pupils and was allowed to develop independently, eventually having its own sixth form.

A new building, Drayton School, on the northern edge of the town replaced Grimsbury in 1973 and eventually became

Father Corrigan, seen at a parish fundraising event, was a leading figure in the campaign for a Roman Catholic secondary school in Banbury.

The Blessed George Napier RC School seen from Addison Road.

an independent comprehensive school. In 1977 more buildings followed on the Easington site for the area Sixth Form Centre, which provided post-16 education for former pupils of Drayton and the Warriner (Bloxham) Schools as well as those already on the campus.

The Harry Judge years laid important foundations that have been built upon by succeeding Principals. By 1993 these subsequent developments had included a Rover-sponsored learning centre, a European Business Centre and a Science-Technology Faculty.

In mid-2002 heartening news for the Blessed George Napier, Drayton and Warriner Schools came from Cherwell District Council in the form of an offer of support for a bid to create specialist college status. Each school would become a centre of excellence for a specific reason: Warriner at Bloxham for IT training, BGN for sports activities and Drayton for technology. Awards of this nature by the central government would almost certainly raise the skill levels of leavers.

At the time of writing, news had just broken to the effect that further buildings may render the original County School building redundant. If this happens educational historians will surely mark this as the end of an era in the town.

From Banbury Tech to Cherwell Valley
The origins of the present college on the Broughton Road have to be sought in the establishment of a Mechanics Institute in Marlborough Road and also in the 1940s

Banbury Technical College woodwork shop in Calthorpe Street.

51 The Green, the College's former Art School and the early home of the Art Society.

central government policy that ensured the rapid expansion of technical education in the renamed Technical Institute.

In 1949 Heads of Engineering, Commerce and Art were appointed and classes for which they were responsible were organised in different parts of the town. A widening of the courses on offer was made possible when a three-year lease on premises at Alcock's yard in North Bar Place made it possible to embrace tuition in building crafts.

Meanwhile the first home of Commerce was 65 High Street, a building that also contained the District Bank. Here a tortoise stove heated a L-shaped room and the space resounded to the clatter of typewriters and a stentorian voice on a gramophone that said 'carriage REETURRN'. It was in this room that a young Jane Cowan addressed the task set by HMIs, namely that commerce classes needed a radical overhaul.

The same review by the inspectors contained adverse comment on the home for art, 51 The Green. They dubbed it 'rather makeshift' though in a much later survey the building's Georgian character was at last appreciated.

The need for a single site for college operations was very clear, and its gover-

nors suggested acquiring some five acres of land close to the Broughton Road that were owned by the builder W.S. Orchard of Bridge Bank in Grimsbury.

It was here that the college took shape, and by June 1953 the Bath Road premises were ready for occupation. However, as Jane Cowan whimsically observed 'it was some time before the local chimney sweep could be persuaded not to exercise his greyhounds on the site'.

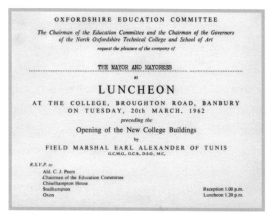

A milestone for the College, the opening of the new college buildings in 1962.

New College buildings after the opening in 1962. The college theatre is on the right.

A turning point for the college came in 1962 during Norman Pratt's time as principal when Earl Alexander of Tunis opened the long-awaited new buildings, which included a communal block, a library and the College Theatre. These facilities enabled staff and students to be

Education at the North Oxon Technical College –
Eric Cordy of the Building and Engineering
department with a construction class.

part of the wider community. In particular, the Banbury Cross Players were pleased to be able to perform 'in a theatre worthy of the town'.

The early 1960s new buildings served the college well. The refectory did excellent business in the days before the town was dominated by sandwich bars and the fast food outlets that replaced earlier generations of cafés.

The College Theatre was multi-purpose, recreational activities by day and major town events in the evenings and at weekends. Few who attended a New Year's Eve Tropical Heat Rave will forget the sight of the college principal dressed as a cannibal chief complete with grass skirt and bone through the nose! At other times of the year there were student hops and delightful summer balls.

The college's interest in agriculture began with a day release class in the 1950s and then grew substantially from the early 60s onwards under the direction of John Cooke. Development of the Mewburn Road unit (now housing fledgling research businesses) was a just reward for the endeavours of John and his staff.

The School of Art developed its sense of independence and strong identity during its tenure of 51 The Green. A move to Broughton Road on an attractive sloping site opposite the main college buildings took place in 1969. Here courses flourished under the inspirational leadership of Bill Stanier and reached their climax with the 'End of the Year Show'. High standards of presentation throughout the year

owed much to Bob Pell and to the organisational and teaching skills of Frances Wrench, who moulded the Fashion Department.

School/College co-operation was a recurrent theme under Morris Smith's guidance. The arrival of Harry Judge at Banbury School very much launched this and several joint appointments were part of an attempt to widen educational opportunities for all.

Concern for those who for various reasons had little prospect of employment was reflected in the acquisition of an industrial unit in Thorpe Way. Banbury Young Industry Ltd placed youngsters on the Youth Opportunities Programme. Schemes to provide further education for those with learning disabilities have also blossomed during the last 15 years.

Reorganisations of structure and management and the declining significance of trade training and agriculture have meant the stage has been cleared for initiatives within a national and higher educational context. The new title, Oxford and Cherwell Valley College, reflects these moves. Gone are the days when mergers were always local and never countywide.

THE GREAT OUTDOORS – ACTIVITIES FOR ALL

People's Park

An event of great importance linked to the early years of this century of change from 1905–2005 was the opening of the People's Park, first in 1912 and then again in 1919 when it was taken over by the Borough and land from Neithrop House had been added. This was a classic example of Victorian beneficence as it was largely funded out of a legacy left to the Council by George Ball, a Parsons Street pharmacist.

The initial impression created by the park was of pleasantly wooded rising ground with a willow walk in the western corner and a zigzag path known as the

Coronation Sports in 1911 held on land adjoining the present People's Park.

Listening to the band in what was to become the People's Park.

Crooked Shades that led to a clap gate on the Paradise end of Bath Road.

Early activities, such as the 1911 coronation year children's sports competition, took place on part of the land that was officially opened as a park by Mrs J. Bloomfield in June 1912. Between the wars this amenity was greatly enhanced by the addition of tennis courts, a bowling green that became home to Borough Bowls Club, an aviary and a children's playground and paddling pool. All this was made possible by the acquisition of more land when the Paradise Square properties were condemned and demolished. In October 1931 a new bandstand replaced an earlier rudimentary structure. This had a capacity for 40 musicians and was conveniently situated close to a natural amphitheatre for a substantial audience. Today only the bowling green, the aviary and the children's playground remain, but the bandstand lingers on in the memory, as does a hut where refreshments were served. In recent years the park has come alive again as the venue for town events. Perhaps the most significant of these has been Sunday in the Park, which with the Cockhorse Festival has been regarded as a constituent part of Mayor's Sunday. Care

People's Park showing the War Memorial and the former bandstand.

of the park led to an award of a green flag of excellence in 2001 and there are signs that this could be a stage towards ensuring that the People's Park is once again the green heart of the town to be enjoyed by all.

'Sunday in the Park', a family entertainment programme of music, moves to a different town park each Sunday in summer. The largest of these with origins dating back to the 1930s is Spiceball Park. Here in the early days uniformed brigades paraded, sometimes not without problems because in those days grazing livestock was never too far away. Perhaps because of its central location, but also due to its size, Spiceball has been the scene of the Banbury Show, with its stalls and arena events, and the Banbury Carnival.

Swimming Pools

Before 1939 going for a swim in Banbury meant taking a dip in a pool located

opened it to the public and controlled its use. The Corporation purchased the pool and its surroundings in 1888, but users would not have noticed any changes until 1899 when the baths were brought up to date. Apart from £20 sanctioned in 1926 for repairs and redecoration, nothing further happened until the 1930s when there was an increasing realisation that 'these baths were obsolete in character if not actually dangerous to public health.' Further pressure on the Borough Council came in the form of a petition for a new pool that was signed by some 2,544 people (Banbury's population was just under 14,000 at the 1931 census). By 1937 land off Park Road for this project had been gifted to the town by Joseph Gillett of Woodgreen, whose banking business had long been established in the town. Funding was found from various sources and the pool was constructed to a design of Sidney Hilton, Borough Surveyor. It opened on 23 May 1939 when a display of swimming and diving

between distributary streams of the River Cherwell on land adjacent to the Great Western Railway and north of the bridge. The bath had been in existence since 1868 when the Banbury Recreational Ground and Bathing Company Limited

Banbury Guides and Brownies parade in Spiceball Park in 1935. Horses graze where Spiceball Leisure Centre is now.

A hang glider publicity stunt outside Spiceball Leisure Centre.

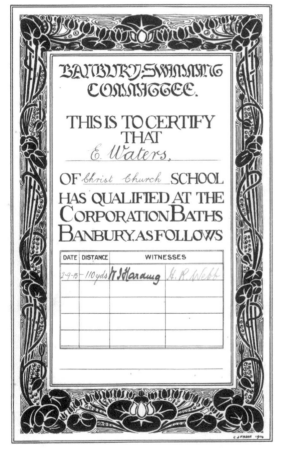

There are few people left who remember swimming in the pool near the Lasher. It was condemned as inadequate and closed in the late 1930s.

and water polo was given by members of the Oxford County Amateur Swimming Association and Oxford University Swimming Club.

Thronged with people on warm summer weekends and alive with enthusiastic supporters of gala events, the outdoor pool has been a part of life in Banbury. Threats to close it in 2005 have been met with strong resistance and much family concern on the part of the present day Gilletts.

The past popularity of outdoor swimming was also demonstrated at the other end of the town in Grimsbury where, during the 1950s especially, the Lido was a welcome surprise at the eastern end of the Middleton Road. A notable feature of the pool was its fountain at one end. Here, apart from the opportunity to take a dip, there were events such as beauty parades, with participants coming mainly from the locality.

Gala events were exciting occasions at the Woodgreen pool. This was the 1957 Schools' Gala, the Mayor, Councillor M. Spokes, has just presented St Mary's Girls with the Junior Shield.

Rival Sports Clubs

By the start of the 20th century Banbury Harriers Athletic Club had impressive status within the town. This was mainly due to the Victorian ideal of providing young men with opportunities for physical exercise. The outcome was a society that participated in a wide range of sports.

Although soccer underdogs to Banbury Spencer FC (formed in 1931), the Harriers took great pride in their appearance on the

A *Banbury Guardian* cartoon by G.D. Coles features a Harriers football match in the 1920s.

field, and their Easington ground (acquired in 1923) was the scene of keen tussles with the likes of Stones Athletic and Oxford Gas.

An extant cricket fixture card for the 1900 season gives some insight into typical encounters. An opening married versus singles match was followed by clashes with village teams like Adderbury and Bloxham, as well as works sides and church sides including Britannia Works CC and St Leonard's Church.

The year 1934 was the 50th anniversary of sports meetings organised by the Harriers. They seem to have attracted quality athletes from clubs such as Birchfield Harriers and Godiva Harriers.

It is perhaps not surprising that the Banbury Harriers have had an impressive list of patrons. These have included Lord North of Wroxton and the industrialist Bernard Samuelson, both of whom were vice-presidents. The annually elected mayor, the Member of Parliament and the Vicar of St Mary's joined them.

Horse racing

In the minds of many people, at the beginning of the 20th century leisure was synonymous with sport. This was certainly true of those people who attended the Crouch Hill races known as the Spring Hunt Meetings.

The last of these was held on Wednesday 24 April 1929 when there were six races. Cheneys printed the race cards on the same day to ensure the greatest accuracy. Riding on that occasion were both professionals and amateurs and included Keith Piggott (father of Lester) and the Wilks brothers, who were Banbury farmers.

The Wroxton chase over two miles got the meeting off to a start at 1.45pm, and

the programme concluded at 4.15pm with the Banbury Cross Local Chase, which was intended for farmers and tradesmen living within a radius of 50 miles of the Cross.

Surviving pictures of Crouch Hill on race day indicate huge crowds. These were not just of local origin. In 1908, for instance, the Great Western Railway advertised a cheap day trip to Banbury from Didcot, Culham, Radley, Abingdon and Oxford in order to enjoy an afternoon at the races organised under distinguished patronage and National Hunt rules. When spectators got thirsty there was a large Hunt Edmunds beer tent to satisfy their needs.

Hunting provided an important link between town and country, especially over the Christmas season. During the 1920s there was an annual 10-mile steeplechase

A once familiar sight in Banbury, huntsmen and hounds meet at Banbury Cross in the early 20th century.

around Christmas time that attracted large crowds. More traditionally, for many years Banbury Cross was a gathering point for the Boxing Day Meet, and as late as 1952 some 1,500 people turned out to see the Warwickshire huntsmen and hounds. Presentation of the stirrup cup also happened outside local hostelries like the Dog and Gun and the White Lion.

Football – Banbury Spencer

Unless the weather was severe local football matches were always part of the programme of Christmas events for the Banbury area. Local derbies were popular. In the 1904–05 season a team of Great Western Railway Servants met a side called Banbury Wanderers. Late in December 1923 Britannia Works FC met Hornton, but on this occasion there was little seasonal goodwill on the field. When a Works team player was sent off for retaliation the *Banbury Guardian* cartoonist made the incident almost theatrical.

For some 35 years the football fortunes of Banbury depended on the playing ability of a works and not a town team. Banbury Spencer FC, formed in 1931, was part of a recreational and social organisation tied to the Britannia Road firm of Spencers.

At the outset and for two years the club engaged in friendly matches before changing its name to Spencer Villa FC and entering the 'C' section of the Oxfordshire Junior League. Success in the 1933–34 season was very much linked to the appointment of Horace Williams as manager. The side topped its section and secured election to the Oxfordshire Senior League under the name of Banbury Spencer.

Before the start of the 1934–35 season the club was invited to take over the fixtures of Rugby Town and play in the Birmingham Combination. By the end of the following season they had managed ninth place out of 19 clubs, a good way to

The Great Western Railway soccer team in 1920–21.

Spencer FC football team in the 1930s.

Spencers had very fine programmes in the 1930s.

greet their new player-coach who was Jimmy Cringen, best known for his FA Cup appearance for Birmingham City against the Baggies (West Bromwich Albion) in 1931.

The early years saw a number of ground changes. Initially matches were played on rented space in the Middleton Road near the Nethercote Turn. The move to the ground where today's successors play took place in 1934. A major advantage of the new location was that the club was able to boast one of the largest ground capacities in the Birmingham League.

Spencers found themselves in some illustrious company, notably the 'A' sides of Aston Villa, West Bromwich Albion, Coventry City and Wolverhampton Wanderers. Unsurprisingly, success was more elusive than it had been.

Easter 1948 was a vintage time for the club. Programme notes were headed 'Gay Puritans at their Best'. Birmingham City Trams, West Bromwich Albion 'A' and Stafford Rangers were all beaten. Thousands flocked to the stadium, the average gate being 2,780 out of a town population of some 14,000 people.

By the 1950s they had achieved a place in the Birmingham Football League. Styled the 'Gay Puritans' the red and gold strip caught the eye of many a compiler of an away venue programme. Banbury's own match day publication included such key historical elements as the 1859 Cross, the lady on a white horse and the body of the Puritan's cat, hanged because of the killing of a mouse on Sunday.

In those times newspaper coverage meant a lot to the club. The *Advertiser* was first with the news on a Wednesday but Thursday's *Guardian* sold 15,000 copies. The compilers of Memory Lane recorded success in competitions such as the Leamington and District League and the Leamington Junior Cup.

The other source of encouragement was the size of gates at the Stadium. In 1953 some 4,150 spectators saw the 2–0 defeat of Oxford City.

Banbury United's Wayne Blossom scores the winning goal during the last minute of extra-time in the play-off match against Sutton Coldfield. This game was the culmination of the very successful 2003–04 season.

Over 700 United fans greeted Wayne's goal knowing that it had clinched promotion from the Dr Martens Eastern Division to the Premier Division of the Southern League. Just a few days earlier Kevin Brocks's side won the Oxfordshire Senior Cup with a 1–0 victory over Oxford United at the Kassam Stadium.

In the mid-60s the Spencer era came to an end and after a short interregnum Banbury United rose from the ashes – at last a town team. United have had a chequered history. Often gates have been meagre compared with the heady days of the Gay Puritans. However, recently, under the direction of Paul Saunders as chairman, the club has been revamped. Promotion to the Premier Division of the Southern League and the avoidance of relegation at the end of last season offered hope that in the future Banbury might again have a team to be feared in non-League football. The players of 2005 travel further to meet current Southern League opposition, but historically it is good to know that they are still the Puritans.

Stones Walking Race

Stones were prominent in Banbury back in the 1920s as printers and furniture manufacturers. Like Spencers, they had a works side in local football. However, they were equally well known for an annual walking race. In 1926, for example, this was held on Saturday 3 July. It started in the Cow Fair near the Town Hall and finished in the Horse Fair. Between these two points competitors followed a route along the Daventry Road to the top of Williamscote Hill, then via Cropredy and Great Bourton to the Southam Road and thus to the Horse Fair. In 1926 a Sgt Millard, who was also the official timekeeper, started the race.

There were some excellent prizes. The winner received a canteen of cutlery, the runner-up a clock, third home got a case of razors and an attaché case was the reward for finishing fourth.

Huge crowds gather in the Horse Fair for Stone's Walking Race.

Stone's Walking Race – a clear winner reaches the final tape close to the Cross.

Local Cricket

Rival clubs are responsible for part of the story of cricket in the Banbury area. Today Banbury CC is well settled into its new home at Bodicote, but a few of the older members may recall early post-war years at Grange Road when visiting teams included company sides like Morris Motors while others represented towns such as Brackley and Buckingham. Banbury Twenty club had its pioneering days in the 1930s on the Daventry Road where an all-round team effort was needed to prepare the wickets and ensure that there was something for the tea interval. Its unusual name derives from the presence of just 20 people at the meeting called to launch the new club.

Earlier in the century, in the summer of 1921, flannelled figures were beginning to flicker to and fro in the newly formed Banbury and District League. There were nine pioneering sides – Bloxham, Broughton and North Newington, Bourton and District, Wroxton and Souldern; the village sides were joined by

Malcolm Spokes (Mayor) batting for the Town Council against the Council Staff in 1957. Jack Friswell is at the non-strikers end.

Banbury Town originals and their wives at their 1967 dinner. The club won a record 18 out of 26 matches in 1967.

Stones Athletic, Blue Bird, Banbury Town Officials and Grimsbury Wesleyans.

During the ensuing years those who played in this league accumulated innumerable and delightful stories about games, grounds and players. George Mepham of Broughton and North Newington recalled a bitterly cold April day at Barford when overcoats replaced whites. He and John Priest were present also on an occasion at Tadmarton when players went prostrate on the ground when a swarm of bees passed over. At yet another match, Gordon Bull, who used to open the batting for Warmington, remembered a lovely warm occasion at the Twyford Seeds ground when a basking adder was removed from the wicket.

The decision to pull up league stumps for the last time has consigned to history such remarkable happenings not to mention performances with bat and ball. A 50 in 15 minutes by Dennis Marles of Broughton and North Newington against Southam will live long in the memory. The Banbury and District League was not short of the game's entertainers. The league was wound up in 2002 but in fact there had been no fixtures since 1993.

Banbury Rugby Club

It is inconceivable that today's well established club should have started in 1925 without a ground to play on, with no funds and with but a handful of possible players. The decision to begin playing rugby was taken in a room over a high street bank. Those present agreed that there were sufficient players to arrange a handful of games against school sides such as All Saints, Bloxham and town teams like Leamington Spa and Stratford-upon-Avon.

Banbury Rugby XV in 1932–33, pictured on the Horton View ground. E.T. Clark, later editor of the *Banbury Guardian*, is on the back row, extreme right.

Two of the enthusiasts at this inaugural gathering were Dr T. Briggs, who had recently joined the Horsefair Surgery, and Mr E.T. Abbotts, of Miller and Abbotts, the local firm of auctioneers. Their first secretary was the popular pork butcher Thomas Hankinson, and it was he who found a ground on the Bloxham Road opposite Springfields. Unfortunately, the land was not without its problems. After heavy rain the field flooded and also there was nowhere for players to change. They had to go all the way to the Bluebird Hotel in Bridge Street and then travel to the ground.

Funds were acquired by arranging an annual ball at the Town Hall. This proved so popular that the event came to be regarded by many as the social event of the winter season. Early balls were 'dress' affairs, and ladies were issued with dance cards and pencils to book their partners. Hundreds of people bought tickets but anxiety set in for the Borough Council who pondered whether or not the ballroom floor would withstand so many feet! However, such a prospect appears not to have worried those who danced to the Lawrence Inn Band or imbibed from the bar provided by the Leathern Bottle.

By 1927 Banbury Rugby Club membership had grown to 60, encouraged by the prospect of playing on a better ground than that discovered by Hankinson. This was at Horton View and became accessible to them because the club joined the Banbury Cricket and Sports Club. As if to celebrate this, annual dinners started to be held at venues such as the White Lion. When the umbrella organisation collapsed in 1937 matches were moved first to the rear of the Horton Hospital and then to a ground halfway to Middleton Cheney.

In 1946 the generosity of the Clark family made it possible for the Rugby Club to secure the lease of the Old Show Ground off the Oxford Road where splendid fetes came to be held. By now the club ran two teams and had a healthy bank balance of some £6,000. Players changed and showered in huts. In 1956 these were replaced by a permanent pavilion and clubhouse.

A notable occasion came in 1959 when the English Rugby Football Union chose Banbury's ground for the first All England trial match. This necessitated making a pitch east to west so that a stand to hold 1,500 people could be erected.

Between 1970 and 1986 the idea of rugby tours took shape, a fourth XV was formed and mini rugby set up, created for boys.

By the time of the 75th anniversary the rugby club had moved to Bodicote Park, and the Old Show Ground was part of history and more pertinently occupied by Sainsburys. Despite recent financial difficulties brought about by a misinterpretation of the rules regarding charitable status, the inspiration for the future should come from the writings of Ted Clark, a past president, 'above all it is the good fellowship to be found among the membership which will continue to be the club's greatest asset as it advances towards its century.'

Banbury's Bowls Clubs

The more leisurely activity of bowls has been dominated by three clubs, Banbury Borough Bowls and the Chestnuts Club on opposite sides of the People's Park and the Central Club that began life on a green behind the Flying Horse in Parsons Street.

Banbury Central Bowls Club's green under construction.

The Chestnuts Club, which celebrated its 200th anniversary in 1980, occupies a green that belonged originally to the Three Tuns (incorporated in the Whately Hall Hotel) on the Horse Fair. Each year this famous old green has been the scene of many notable fixtures, including the meeting with Handsworth Wood Club from Birmingham. Within the Chestnuts, leading retailers and business people have been especially prominent. With some justification it can be said that the club has been at the very heart of the market town.

The Banbury Central Bowling club enjoyed a centenary in 2001. Many enjoyable fixtures marked the years up to 1973 when the club lost its battle to stay 'central' and moved to Horton View. Among these fixtures were some in 1940 when the club agreed to take part in a Hospital League. Proceeds went to the Horton and sides competed for the Keyser

Banbury Chestnuts, formerly Banbury Green Bowls Club.

Early cyclists and motorcyclists outside the George and Dragon in the Horse Fair.

Cup. By the mid-1950s ladies were gracing the green and became involved in some notable events such as the Johns Trophy competition.

Local Wheelers
Down the years Banbury has had many cycling clubs, some of them offshoots of local firms others under the direction of athletic organisations such as the Banbury Harriers. A club dedicated to cycling only and road racing in particular has been the Star Cyclists club. This club was formed in 1891 and is still in existence today. Back in 1936 a typical comment among members was 'anyone fond of cycling and good comradeship should give the joys and delights of club cycling a trial.'

An important event in their calendar was the annual run. In 1930 the route of some 21 miles took in Middleton Cheney, Farthinghoe, Brackley, Croughton, Aynho and Adderbury. Sadly this was not a good year, bad weather and confusion over the course resulted in injuries.

Races had wide support throughout the town. Prizes were made available by many local businesses such as Maycocks (hairdressers) in the High Street, Trinders Toys in Broad Street and Cook's Tobacco Store at the Cross.

Like many other clubs in the town, the club's base was in a public house. Up until 1932 this had always been the White Horse in the High Street, but when the club's long-term secretary A.F. Kilby took over the Dog and Gun in North Bar activities shifted there. This appears to have been a good move as membership

Star cyclists enjoy companionship on a day out.

A group of Star Cyclists pass Grimsbury Co-op – riding bikes covering the reigns of five monarchs.

increased and a growing spirit of enterprise saw the start of Sunday races and the admission of tandem riders to gatherings.

A famous run for motorcyclists

Since 1948 the Banbury Run has been an annual event within the outdoor leisure scene. Organised by the Veteran and Vintage Motor Cycle Club and attracting entries from all over the world, this began as the Birmingham to Banbury Reliability Run. A key part of the programme has always been trials at Sunrising in the Edge Hill area. As Dr Nick Hill rightly commented in 1997, 'Watch the field as they climb to the top – the reward is the sight of lovingly restored old motorcycles in action.' Five years earlier a total of 360 cycles took to the road, the oldest dating back to 1899.

Over the years there has been a notable increase in the scale of this event – 2004 attracted over 500 entrants – a factor in the choice of a local venue as the base area. The Horse Fair livestock market, Castle Gardens Car Park and Drayton School have all been used and for a few years in the 1990s the event was held at Towcester Race Course, a most unpopular move.

Two fascinating aspects of the 1967 Run were that the class for very early machines attracted the then oldest running motor cycle in the world, an 1898 Werner, and also that one of the late entrants in this class was Bill Moore who rode at

Lady rider in the Banbury Run *c*.1952.

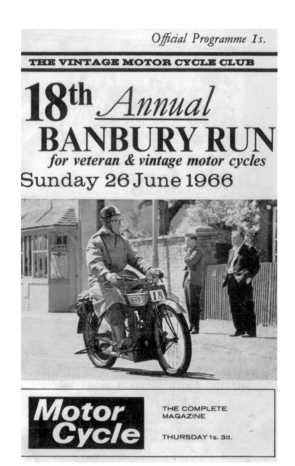

Official programme for the 18th Annual Banbury Run in 1966, which attracted an entry of 351 bikes, including one from the US.

Banbury Cross, the start point for a round of the British Rally Championship in 2002.

Brooklands before 1914. In 1992 Cropredy riders John Atkins and Geoff Parratt were successful on their 1927 Humber machines that had consecutive number plates. By 1998 John Quincey of Banbury was an established entrant with machines that included a 1926 Triumph and Gloria sidecar. He was part of the 50th anniversary run that helped to make June a notable month in the Banbury and District sporting calendar.

Fetes and Festivals
The Hospital Fete

The Horton Hospital Fete was a remarkable event, especially in the 1930s when thousands lined the streets to see the procession of floats. Apart from the astonishing length of this procession, the fete attracted a lot of attention because it was a composite affair. There was a band or bands, numerous sideshows and performances of various kinds by quality entertainers.

The fete of 1937 was the 14th such occasion, and, like the others, it was organised by the Banbury and District Workpeople's Association. Entries of floats for the procession assembled in Bath Road and West Bar, but it was not until the Cross was reached that spectators were able to observe the crowning of the Carnival King, who was John Cheney, the Mayor in this, George VI's Coronation Year.

The day was a very full one. It was interspersed with dancing and keep fit displays, punctuated by a band contest for which spectators were asked 'to preserve a discreet silence' and topped up with the music of Ken Prewer and his Premiere Orchestra, who played for dancing on the Nurses' lawn, which was illuminated by the SWS Electric Company Ltd.

Local businesses were generous in their support for an event that raised much needed funds for their hospital.

A 1930s Hospital Fete procession passes the Cross.

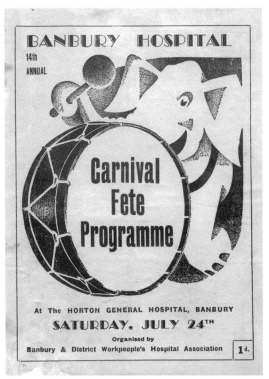

The Carnival Fete programme, the Carnival procession attracted thousands.

Throughout the afternoon and evening you could keep cool with a Walls ice cream, spend a shilling on a tea in the Co-operative Society tent and raise or recharge your glass in the White Hart's somewhat larger tent. Other attractions and sideshows included Edward and Sons' fun fair, which was located in a field at the rear of the hospital, Edward and Kench's wheel of fortune, Banbury Spencer's supervised goal kicking and a darts competition courtesy of the Great Western Railway locomotive employees.

The highlight of the occasion was the special programme involving professional artistes provided by Harry Daubney's Variety Agency. Their exotic names included Les Ferrantis, Anton and the Orlandos – balancers, jugglers and acrobats. There was also that evergreen favourite, the Punch and Judy show.

A talent competition ensured that there

was some spectator participation, and Tom Hutchings provided piano support for this.

On the back of the fete programme, which cost 1d, there appeared a happy, smiling, well-groomed man lifting his pint of Hunt Edmunds' Banbury Cross Ale. I am sure he was celebrating a jolly good event that successfully raised a lot of money for a good cause.

The Rugby Club Fete

Apart from their considerable contribution to sport in the area, the Banbury Rugby Club organised a fete on August Bank Holiday Monday that was eagerly awaited by large numbers of people. It

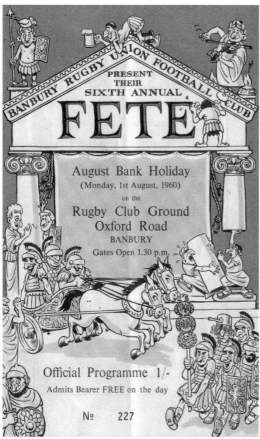

Banbury Rugby Club's sixth annual fete in August 1960. It was the policy of the club to donate a percentage of the fete profits to charitable organisation, particularly local ones. From the previous three fetes £600 was shared out among 21charities.

first entered the town's calendar of social events back in 1955 when members of the club saw the opportunity to raise much-needed funds. Beneficiaries were local charities such as the Banbury Invalid Tricycle Association and the District Scouts.

Band of the Royal Marines marching up the Oxford Road on their way to the Rugby Club Fete of August 1962.

The programme was always enterprising. In 1960 the centrepiece of the fete itself was an arena with a succession of attractions culminating in a display of 'Beating the Retreat' by the Scots Guards.

Overall the scale of the event was impressive and was certainly matched by the raffle. First prize that year was a Vespa scooter, a good return on a 6d (2p) ticket.

The fun did not end with the announcement of the winners as from 9.00pm to 2.00am you could join the grand flannel dance to the music of the Ken Martin Band at the Crown Hotel in Bridge Street.

Two years later the fete attracted thousands, so many that supplies of ice cream ran out and there was a bar crisis – getting a glass was one thing but getting something to put in it was another! On the positive side the Coldstream Guards played lively music, slices of roast ox were on offer and Alderman Braggins top hat

The fifth Annual Cockhorse Festival will coincide with Mayor's Sunday.

would be held in the People's Park and be part of the occasion known as 'Mayor's Sunday in the Park'. Children were encouraged to make and bring along their own steeds and the best ones were awarded a prize. In the period before the festival itself the spirit of the occasion was captured by the presence of three 'Banbury in Bloom' floral Cockhorses at the Cross and by a delightful variant on the rhyme itself:

> Ride a Cockhorse to Banbury town
> It's four hundred years since they pulled the Cross down.
> See capering creatures of weird design
> Greet the return of the Lady Fine.

Since that year each successive Town Mayor has featured the festival in the overall programme of civic events and participants come from all over the world to join in.

was the Aunt Sally target – especially for his political opponents.

Cockhorse Festival

In April 2002 the events outlook for the forthcoming summer was that it would be 'a vintage one if your interest is in Banbury traditions'. Simon Pipe, known to many for his work with BBC Radio Oxford and his connection with local Morris Dancers, was busy working on a new initiative for celebrating Banbury's renowned nursery rhyme (Ride a Cock Horse). His vision was a festival during which teams of jockeys would ride six huge hobbyhorses made by students of the North Oxfordshire College. The races

Hobby Horse Festival 2003.

INDOOR LEISURE –
SOMETHING FOR EVERYONE

During the last 100 years going out in the Banbury area has meant many different things to many people. An early 1940s survey of life in the parishes between Banbury and Chipping Norton revealed the extent to which leisure hours revolved around a village hall where occasional dances were held, but more particularly the pub where men especially gathered 'to drink a little beer and play darts.'

The Big Band era
The young at heart were drawn to bigger social occasions in the market town. An important source of attraction from the 1920s onwards was the 'big band' sound. Someone who supplied this in abundance

Ken Prewer band at Wincotts Ballroom, South Bar.

Dancing at Wincott's ballroom.

was Ken Prewer who, along with his musicians, entertained a generation of dance band devotees in North Oxfordshire.

Back in the 1930s they met for rehearsals at Ivy House in South Bar. The stalwarts were Arthur Bowton, Dick Wise (who was to form a rival band later), Tom Brinkworth, Frank Bolton, Ron Grubb, 'Hodgy' Perkins and Beryl Pewsey.

Christmas was the time for fancy dress

Brownie Lay, with female admirers, started out as Ken Prewer's drummer before forming his own very successful band.

balls with dancing to live bands. On 20 December 1923 some 200 people turned up at the Town Hall for the Nomads Ball. About half of these had invested in outfits that were that little bit special, such as a Persian princess or a cavalry colonel. A year later, in the words of the *Banbury Guardian*, 'Indian Chiefs danced with Puritan Maids'.

Many companies held their own dances at Christmas. In 1940 employees of the surgical appliances firm Spencers crowded into Wincotts Ballroom for exhibitions of tap dancing, accordion solos and above all the distinctive sounds of the Brownie Lay Band.

By the 1950s Ken Prewer and his orchestra were heavily in demand over the festive season. Patrons were able to take to the floor of the Town Hall on Christmas Eve, Boxing Night and on New Year's Eve. During the 1940s and 1950s the band also appeared regularly at Wincotts Ballroom in South Bar and at the Winter Gardens, just off the High Street. In addition, there were numerous one-off appearances at a host of venues. During the golden years at Wincotts Ballroom, evenings were often diversified by competitions – typical was that for 'sweater girls'.

Ken's greatest enthusiasm was for strict tempo style dancing, and this meant he was in demand for such events as Hunt Balls and on occasion to provide support to legendary bands such as Victor Sylvester.

In October 1960 regulars on the dance floor were left to treasure memories of 'Who's taking you home tonight' and 'You're dancing on my heart' when Ken decided to hang up his saxophone. On 27 October 1960 the *Banbury Guardian* carried the simple message 'we regret to announce the retirement of Ken Prewer', a regret shared by a whole host of people in Banbury and the district.

The post-Prewer years were filled by Brownie Lay, Ken's drummer, who carried on the tradition for live dance music locally. Like Ken, he was very flexible. At the Victuallers' Banquet and Ball of 1962 his light orchestra played Cole Porter and Jerome Kern melodies during the dinner, but then it was 'over to you Brownie' for a programme of dance music. In later years his regular haunt was the Whately Hall where dinner dances filled Saturday nights in a good many diaries.

Jazz at the Mount

A very different kind of musical entertainment was provided by the Banbury Jazz Club, which was formed in 1967 when it met in the Cellar Bar of the Mount Hotel (now the Oxford House Hotel). People

Banbury Jazz Club's founder/hon organiser and well-known local tenor sax man Pete Lay in action on the 'Opening Night' of the Club in October 1967, in the 'Cellar Bar' of the Mount Hotel (now Bar 27 of the Banbury House Hotel).

John Dankworth, the legendary alto-sax great – one of the many top jazz musicians who have appeared at the Banbury Jazz Club over the years. He played at the club's 31st and 33rd October 'anniversary nights' in 1998 and 2000.

were introduced to the Peter Lay (son of Brownie) Quartet. Terry Mortimer played the piano, Eddie James supplied the base effect and the late Ron Mole was drummer.

Once jazz was in the frame the aim of the club was to present local and midlands musicians together with the occasional top British and American recording stars. No wonder that, on the occasion of the 20th anniversary, Ted Hanson wrote in *Banbury Focus* 'expect a real humdinger of a session on 20 October'.

Folk Clubs

Another club that achieved a high profile within its own musical orbit was a Folk Club that was launched at the Prince of Wales pub in Centre Street, Grimsbury, in November 1974. Back in the 1850s and 1860s this beerhouse had been the focal point of an annual Wakes Week of drinking and making merry, but over 100 years on very different sounds fill its meetings room. Regular folk evenings were the outcome of activities involving enthusiastic stalwarts. These included John Leslie, Chris Leslie (now of Fairport Convention), Bryan Sheppard, Barry Worsley, Sheena Powell and Tim and Ann Radford. Usually it was their warm-up efforts that got evenings underway and established an ambience for guest artists who appeared under such evocative titles as 'Spreadthick', 'Mr Gladstone's Bag' and the 'Armpit Jug Band'. This last named group produced a unique and exciting blend of authentic jug, folk-blues and good-time music. It was just this kind of entertainment that ensured that the club could stand alongside the earlier and rival General Foods Club.

Chris (left) and John Leslie, founder members of the Prince of Wales Folk Club, performing at the 30th anniversary concert held at the Mill on 20 April 2005.

The Armpit Jug Band first entertained folk enthusiasts at the Prince of Wales Folk Club in the 1970s. They returned to play at the Mill in 2005 as part of the 30th anniversary celebrations.

In 1978 the club left its original home and appeared at a number of venues, mostly pubs, notably the Unicorn, Wheatsheaf, Jolly Weavers and the Reindeer.

Today some of those founder members responsible for getting things going at the Prince of Wales are members or appear as entertainers at the Banbury Folk Club that meets in the Mill Arts Centre, and Spiceball Park and the Armpit Jug Band, who are still going strong, top the bill on special occasions.

The Winter Gardens

From the early 1960s the Winter Gardens off the Cross end of the High Street was Banbury's outstanding entertainment centre for over 20 years. The Winter Gardens was not only a dance Mecca but also the indoor leisure venue for many

The interior of the Winter Gardens, used for concerts, dances, wrestling, roller skating and exhibitions.

A Police Ball in 1956, a grand start to life at the Winter Gardens.

diverse attractions. Apart from roller skating nights, there were boxing contests and wrestling matches. Large exhibitions, in particular a Banbury version of the Ideal Home Exhibition, were also staged there. Undoubtedly, the main reason for its success was Banbury's legendary impresario Ethel Usher who welcomed stars such as Acker Bilk, Joe Loss and the Rolling Stones. Sadly, she is equally remembered for her rejection of an appearance by the Beatles because they wanted a fee of £500. Wrestling matches

Programme for the third Ideal Home Exhibition to be sponsored by the Banbury Chamber of Trade at the Winter Gardens. It included fashion shows, demonstrations and trade exhibits.

were very popular. Dale Martin Promotions Ltd in association with Ethel Usher offered evenings of irresistible bouts. Typically, in March 1962 the Mexican Thunderbolt met Essex's Teenage Idol.

Banbury School of Dancing celebrates its Silver Jubilee. Mary Barratt (née Trump), centre, with husband Roy on her right and the Mayor and Mayoress, Councillor and Mrs Fred Blackwell, on her left.

Schools of Dancing

On 24 July 1937 the many people who attended the Horton Hospital Fete were treated to a memorable display of dancing. This took place on the front lawn of the nurses' hostel and was given by pupils of the Margaret Jane Dancing Studio.

Sixteen years later Mary Trump launched the Banbury School of Dancing in premises at North Bar. It had been her ambition to do this even though much of her previous work had been in cabaret with the occasional appearance in pantomime at theatres such as the Bristol Hippodrome.

Mary trained at the Margaret Pemberton Dancing Academy in Banbury and then went to ballet school full time in Bristol. This may well have prepared her for the way ahead, which was rarely easy. In an interview for the *Banbury Guardian* during her school's Silver Jubilee year she remarked 'I can hardly believe I have clocked up 25 years. It's been a hard and wonderful career and we have made a great many friends'.

After 24 years Mary Barrett, née Trump, presented silver medallist Peter Hillman with an engraved cup to mark the fact that he was the 9,000th successful pupil. It was her most treasured hope that this figure could be advanced to 10,000 by the time of a magnificent Jubilee Ball in the Winter Gardens off the High Street. Not only was this achieved but also she and her husband secured their first successes in a new examination for the Viennese Waltz.

Down the years the school did a lot of demonstration work in ballet and tap, and some of the most memorable events were with 200 children on stage at the College Theatre.

Other dancing schools have followed suit. In particular, the Suzanne School of Dancing has been seen to good effect with organisations like the Banbury Operatic Society.

In March 1988 the *Banbury Guardian* reported that the Joanne Mills School of Dance had produced an amazing display at a sell-out show. 'The audience was completely razzled and dazzled', and bemused when two of her pupils danced with biscuit tins attached to their feet.

Theatre

In the *Banbury Guardian* from 1 October 1953 J. Cashman recalled the 62 years of the New Theatre in Church Lane. Performances there stretched from *Don Juan* in 1798 to Shakespeare's *As You Like it* in 1861.

Far less well known was the Eden Theatre in Grimsbury, for which advertisements appeared in the *Banbury Guardian* during the early years of the last century. These afford some positive clues as to the nature of this theatre. It was a portable building located in the cricket field behind the Cricketers beerhouse in the Middleton Road.

Horace Whitmee, the manager, appears to have aimed at diversity in the programme with 'nothing at which the most susceptible could take offence'. Stage plays were given nightly performances and included such titles as *the Blind Girl of Paris* and *the Dumb Man of Manchester*. In February 1903 Whitmee appears to have captured something of a scoop for his large and appreciative audiences. *Secrets of the Police* was described as sensational drama, entirely new to Banbury.

The Eden Theatre seems to have had a

Vicars in Panto at Church House in 1970. Church House was home to many amateur dramatic groups including the Banbury Cross Players. It is now the Church House Bistro.

short life as live theatres go, and any further stage performances for the Banbury public appear to have depended on bookings by the managers of the Exchange in the Market Place (a former Corn Exchange). Occasional live shows continued to be presented in this building after its conversion first to Blinkhorn's Picture Palace (1907) and then the Palace Cinema (1926).

Elsewhere in Banbury amateur drama performances lured people out of their homes. In the years before World War Two a group of well-known local people with Methodist connections performed on a small stage at Church House in the Horse Fair. On the occasion of their production called *Passing Brompton Road*, the *Banbury Guardian* featured a series of caricatures of the principal artists.

Christmas entertainment in the Banbury area has nearly always included something with a seasonal flavour. In 1922 Blinkhorns Picture Palace presented a grand musical novelty revue with the topical title *Crackers – a Bon-Bon of delight in two pulls and a bang*. Patrons

paid between 9d (just under 4p) and 2s (10p) to see it. Three years later, after the theatre had changed its name to the Palace, the new management staged its first pantomime with sets for 12 scenes and a cast of 30 artists. More ambitious still was the orchestra whose leaders had been engaged from London. Tickets for this ranged from as little as 6d (2p) to 2s 4d (around 12p).

Banbury Cross Players

Just before VE Day the Banbury Cross Players Society was formed. Their first public performance, seen free of charge in Bloxham School's Great Hall, was Noel Coward's *Hay Fever*. Just how much the Players owed to contemporary and partly contemporary organisations is difficult to say for certain. The Old Banburians Dramatic Society (past Banbury Grammar School pupils) contain a number of names common to both – Graham Wilton, Sonia Blinkhorn and Richard Briggs are typical examples.

That the Society has survived to celebrate its 60th anniversary in 2005 may

The cast of *An Ideal Husband* presented at the town hall in 1951.

seem remarkable in the light of early difficulties highlighted in local newspapers. In 1949 both Owen Reid, Town Clerk and the Players' chairman, and Mary Cheney, the then Mayor of Banbury, appealed for more support to save the Banbury Cross Players from going under for financial reasons. There were also the dodgy electrics at Church House, key members of the cast cut off by extreme weather conditions and rehearsal rooms (the only premises they could call their own) burning down.

Banbury Cross Players Jill Smith and Pat Andrews, as the Ugly Sisters, entertain the elderly occupants of Lincoln House in 1977.

It was also in 1949 that Andrew Campbell, who was editor of the periodical *Civic Entertainment,* gave a lecture about civic theatres to an audience at the Crown Hotel in Bridge Street. He spoke about co-operation between civic and education authorities leading to visits from touring companies sponsored by the Arts Council. Despite his insistence that

towns the size of Banbury should have a multi-purpose building to house such events, nothing came of his visit.

The Banbury Cross Players had always campaigned for a purpose-built theatre and enthusiastically supported the ill-fated project to turn Church House into the Jimmy Black Theatre, but the nearest the town had come to it was with the opening in 1964 of the North Oxfordshire Technical College's Broughton Road site that included a College theatre. Even then in this new home there were many low points for the Players when rows of empty seats faced those appearing on stage. Most popular with the public were comedies and Christmas pantos and also outdoor performances staged at local stately homes such as those in the grounds of Broughton Castle and Wroxton Abbey. It was at the latter that Martin Blinkhorn, styled by the *Banbury Guardian* as 'master amateur showman', intrigued theatregoers with his staging of the *Comedy of Errors.* The newspaper critic's words really caught the eye, 'if you can work out why there is a firing squad and a chorus of nuns not to mention a drunken doctor and a speaking tube – then you are probably as mad as the BCP team who are working like maniacs to produce a riotous evening of fun!'

Martin Blinkhorn was also very much part of the pantomime scene, both as a writer and performer. In the early 1950s, before the opening of the College Theatre, pantos were staged at Church House in the Horse Fair. Here the Banbury Cross Players put on productions that, in the words of the *Banbury Guardian*, had glamour, dancing, colour and spectacle along with that essential characteristic of good old-fashioned gusto. In 1953 *Red Riding Hood* with Martin Blinkhorn and Pat Butler in the cast was 'briskly paced, warm and folded itself right round the very responsive audiences'. Musical support for the players came especially from that local virtuoso performer on the piano and organ Tom Hutchings.

The renovation and development of the Mill in Spiceball Park has opened up a whole new range of cultural opportunities, largely fulfilling the brief for a civic theatre set down by Andrew Campbell in 1949 over 20 years earlier.

The Mill

In the early 1970s Oxfordshire County Council bought a large building in Spiceball Park that had once been Lamprey's flourmill. The purpose was to provide people in Banbury and district with new facilities for arts and entertainment and also to devote a substantial space to the operation of a club for young people.

By 1983 the *Banbury Focus*, an independent free newspaper later closely allied with the *Banbury Guardian*, was able to write enthusiastically about a home for the Mill Drama Group, which would be a venue for the Mill Folk Club, a fully equipped photographic darkroom, a gymnasium for weight lifting and various meetings. Seven years later the *Focus* had changed its name to the *Citizen* and was sporting a weekly column for a guest writer. On 18 January 1990 this spot was filled by some exciting news of building work at the Mill supplied by Tony Snee, its Warden. The paper's caption was 'The Mill – it will be worth coming off the M40 for.' The focus of everyone's attention was

The Mill Theatre, home to the Folk Club and the Banbury Cross Players.

the revamping of the theatre, good news for all users and especially the Banbury Cross Players who had found a settled home at last. Snee remarked that 'adventure, creativity and a sense of value give life to a community. We aim to offer some of that at the Mill and we are proud of what has been achieved so far.'

Amateur Operatics

Dickie Briggs was also early on the scene with the Banbury Amateur Operatic Society. This group of enthusiasts evolved from performances of the *Pirates of Penzance*, a joint Banbury Cross Players and Easington Modern Boys School production. Pioneers of this move towards opera were Stanley and Gladys Blackler, who wanted to bring together those whose interests were within song and dance.

Ruth Hartwell (Ruth, Pirate maid of all work) and Tom Pratt (Sgt of Police) in *Pirates of Penzance*.

Founder member Gareth Jeremy as Chief Sitting Bull in *Annie Get Your Gun* in the millennium year.

The local press came out with rave reviews. Typical expressions in the *Guardian* were 'gay and colourful' and 'Gladys really made it tick'. The front page for 22 June features a photograph of the women in the opera and then provided a classic caption of 'all is lost for the pirates when they meet up with this bevy of beauty on the sea shore.'

The cast of *Pirates of Penzance* included many of those on whom this successful society came to depend:

SAM:	Gareth Jeremy
PIRATE KING:	Stan Blackler
FREDERICK:	Fred Prescott
RUTH:	Ruth Hartwell
EDITH:	Della Hawkins
KATE:	Sally Warwick
ISOBEL:	Stella Fairbairn
MABEL:	Gladys Blackler
MAJ-GEN STANLEY:	Dick Briggs
POLICE SERGEANT:	Thomas Pratt

In the chorus were names that were soon to become familiar to Banbury audiences such as June Charles, Nan Turner, Adrian Hearn and Paul Blencowe.

Between 1961 and 2005 there have been many fine productions, mostly staged at Banbury School's Wykham Hall (the former Boys Modern). High points were reached in the Millennium year with that Wild West extravaganza *Annie Get Your Gun* and *Merry England* presented in the grounds of Broughton Castle. I am sure that the Blacklers would have drawn huge satisfaction that their leap in the dark in 1961 had turned into this exciting programme for 2000.

Banbury Choral Society

On 4 February 1942 the *Guardian* and *Advertiser* newspapers both announced that a decision had been taken to form a choral society under the auspices of the Education Committee of the Banbury Co-operative Society Ltd. They added that Geoffrey Furnish, well known as a pianist in local music circles, would be the conductor.

Each year the Society took part in an established annual Festival, the climax of which was a concert, and that of 1946 surely would have lived on in the memory because the soloist was that remarkable contralto Kathleen Ferrier. In his booklet about the Society called We *are the Music Makers*, Walter Cheney has commented 'those who heard her sing on Saturday night, the thousands who have heard her sing, and the tens of thousands who will hear her, are deeply indebted to the teacher who first realised the latent possibilities of a truly wonderful voice.'

However, the dedication of local people also illuminated the Choral Society's performances. Between 1952 and 1964 the accompanist at rehearsals was Ena Grubb, an outstanding teacher who taught at least three generations of Banburians to play the piano.

During World War Two the choir brought music to mass audiences, lifting spirits and raising funds for local charities. A typical example was in July 1943 when some of the singers took part in a concert organised by the Co-operative Society's 'Holiday's at Home' committee. This also supported the Horton Hospital and the Red Cross Prisoners of War fund.

Five years later the Banbury Choral Society rendered Elgar's *Dream of Gerontius* in front of an 800-strong audience in St Mary's Church in the Horse Fair. The Society had come a long way, as indeed had Geoffrey Furnish himself.

Following his death in 1974, Geoffrey was succeeded first by Malcolm Sargent, who was also the founder and first

Banbury Co-operative Choral Society performs *The Dream of Gerontius* in February 1948 under their conductor Geoffrey Furnish.

Rehearsal of St Matthew Passion in 1992, the 50th anniversary performance under Eddie Palmer.

conductor of the Banbury Symphony Orchestra, and then in 1976 by Eddie Palmer, a teacher at Magdalen College, Brackley. Eddie Palmer is credited especially with bringing stability to the society at a difficult time and of establishing the same high standards of singing as those exacted by Geoffrey Furnish.

Outside of such performances the choir

has played a significant wider role in community events such as those planned by the Lions Club of Banbury. A good example of this was at the Christmases of 1990 and 1991 when the choir provided the essential nucleus of carol singers at Broughton Castle. Carols by torchlight were sung in the courtyard. It is hardly surprising, therefore, that in her foreword to *We are the Music Makers* Mariette Saye, writing from the castle, noted that 'there is no doubt that the Choral Society is a strengthening force in the life of the town and we are proud of our choir'.

Lions' Music Hall

An annual event that brought together some of the best of local entertainers was the Old Time Music Hall. Based on the Leeds variety show made famous by tele-

Lions Music Hall at North Oxfordshire Technical College (Oxford and Cherwell Valley College).

vision, this used to pack the College Theatre for at least three nights in April. It was a collaborative venture by the Lions and Rotary clubs of Banbury in aid of some very worthy causes. A glance down the list of support people in a programme of 1970 reveals some local legendary names including Alf Grant, who was a pianist in the Brownie Lay Band, and Tom Hutchings, organist at St John's RC Church for over 60 years, who frequently kept social occasion audiences happy with his distinctive presentations.

Cinema in Banbury

In 1996 the Post Office had a commemorative stamp issued to mark 100 years of going to the cinema. This should have reminded Banbury people that the town had once had three dream palaces.

Blinkhorns Picture Palace was the outcome of converting a former Corn Exchange in the Market Place way back in 1907. Payments of 4d (2p), 7d (3p) and 1s (5p) admitted you to silent movies. In the 1920s this cinema was renamed the Palace and then became part of the ABC circuit. It was here that Tom Byrne was not only manager but sufficient of a personality to be known affectionately as Uncle Tom. After 20 years of service the curtain fell on the last film showing for which he was responsible, and the *Banbury Guardian* burst into verse: 'From time to time the curtain opens to the closing of the show, we've known a friend when times were good as well as when they're slow.' The final flickering of the silver screen was that Albert Finney classic *Saturday Night and Sunday Morning*.

The Palace Cinema, formerly Blinkhorns Picture Palace.

Pace and Bowden, humorists, appeared at Blinkhorns Picture Palace in 1911.

A second small cinema with facilities for a stage was built in Broad Street and opened in 1911. This was the Grand, which was enlarged to 680 seats after a fire in 1931. At the time of the Coronation of King George VI this cinema gave a 16-page souvenir filled with royal photographs to all patrons. It was in the time of E.A. Bagley, possibly the Grand's best-known manager. The unique world to which he admitted cinemagoers was characterised by usherettes with their torch-light search for empty seats and the haze of cigarette smoke that filled the space between the front row and the screen.

When the Palace closed, the ABC Minors' programme of Saturday morning presentations switched to the Grand. Youngsters queued along Pepper Alley to be admitted through the back door. This

The Ken Prewer Band on a Hospital Fete float advertise the mid-1930s hit musical film, *The Music Goes Round*.

158

The former Grand Cinema, now the Chicago Rock Café.

was known as the 'Rush'. In December 1968 the very last film could not have had a more appropriate title, *Where were you when the lights went out?* Journalist Ted Hanson had the answer when he cheekily remarked 'playing bingo'.

Banbury's third cinema opened on the eve of World War Two and was known as the Regal. Like the Grand, it was designed to permit stage performances as well as film shows. Name changes have caused Banburians to adjust to Essoldo and then a Canon Cinema. The Odeon group took over a twinned building, the second screen being formed from the former stalls and circle in the early 1970s. The fulfilment of its slogan 'fanatical about films' has resulted in the emergence of special showings of blockbusters and the highly successful Senior Screen on Wednesday

mornings with coffee and biscuits provided. These moves have ensured the cinema's survival in times beyond the real threat of a local multiplex in the town.

Banbury and District Art Society

This society emerged in 1947 out of a background of economic austerity and despite the bleakness of that year's winter. Its formation, like so many other groups, owed much to a few enthusiasts, and these included Joseph Ferrers, who had been appointed head of the Banbury School of Art in 1946, Jane Cowan of Banbury Tech, Tom Muskett, borough librarian, Geoffery Furnish, Co-op Choir, J.C. Frost, art teacher at Banbury Grammar School and Horton Smith of Stones the printers.

In the early years virtually the only activity was the annual exhibition held at 65 High Street, the home of Banbury Technical Institute's Department of Commerce. As time went on, and under the promotional influence of Norman Pratt (Institute Head), the society diversified into hosting other exhibitions, accommodating one-man shows and putting on Arts Council exhibitions and collections of paintings borrowed from places such as Broughton Castle. Opening days could be enlivened by the presence of people like Sacheverell Sitwell and E.H. Shepard (illustrator of the works of A.A. Milne, including *Winnie the Pooh*).

As membership grew between 1947 and 1967 a wider programme emerged that included visits, lectures and discussions. The society gathered momentum, especially under the stimulus of the Bob Pell master class at the Banbury College.

The annual exhibition has had many homes including the old art school building, 51 The Green, a fine Georgian house where members encountered a battle for display space, and also, from 1969, they could obtain the ultimate prize of securing the Barnden Trophy for the best entry.

In 1997 the society celebrated 50 years with a special exhibition in Banbury Town Hall. By then the Bob Pell master classes were but a distant memory, but the society's show was firmly established in the social calendar of the town.

Banbury Historical Society

The Banbury Historical Society grew out of a series of talks about the town given by Dr E.R.C. (Ted) Brinkworth in the autumn of 1957. These well attended lectures called 'New Light on Old Banbury' gave Ted and Jeremy Gibson, great grandson of the founder of Stones printing business, the opportunity to explore the idea of a historical society at a time when such bodies were uncommon outside universities.

They and 16 others agreed a programme of monthly lectures that attracted other people to join the new society. Within a year over a hundred had paid subscriptions and among the

Members of the Banbury Historical Society at an exhibition in the Town Hall with the Mayor and Mayoress, Councillor Malcolm Spokes and Mrs Spokes during the Mayoral year 1957–58. Founder member Jeremy Gibson, extreme right, President Lord Seye and Sele, centre.

Dr Ted Brinkworth (centre) talks to Gwen Bustin, Alderman and registrar at Banbury Grammar School. The Banbury Historical Society grew out of a very successful series of local history lectures given by Dr Brinkworth.

subscribers, as a corporate member, was the *Banbury Guardian*.

That first year was a busy one with a group of members working on transcribing Parish Registers, others taking part in an excavation of the castle mound, the first edition of the society's magazine *Cake and Cockhorse* was being eagerly read and, in the autumn of 1959, the long-heralded publication of the first records volume *An index to wills proved in the Peculiar Court of Banbury 1542–1859* went ahead.

Since then the Society has gone from strength to strength with over 250 members worldwide and members support lectures at Banbury Museum and a programme of summer visits in considerable numbers. The main purpose of the Society is to encourage an interest in the history of 'Banburyshire'. To this end, 28 records volumes and over 100 issues of *Cake and Cockhorse* have been published, and past *Cake and Cockhorses* are now available on CD-Rom to facilitate this research.

OUR HORTON

In 1997 the Horton Hospital celebrated 125 years of provision of medical services for the people of Banbury and district. It was a year in which to reflect on the founder, Mary Ann Horton. Back in 1869 she decided to devote her money to almshouse construction in Middleton Cheney and to the establishment of an infirmary in Banbury. Miss Horton had inherited financial resources from her father, William, who had made his fortune from the invention of an elastic yarn crucial to the manufacture of silk stockings.

Sadly, Mary died in the same year that she made this momentous decision. However, her nephew, John Henry Kolle, ensured the fulfilment of his aunt's wishes and set aside £10,000 for the building work on a site in the Oxford Road.

The hospital was opened by the Bishop of Oxford on 17 July 1872 and contained

The original Horton Infirmary, now mainly offices. The building is grade II listed.

20 beds as well as a dispensary. The latter enabled working-class people to secure medical treatment by payment of a weekly sum of 1d per person or 3d (just over 1p) for a whole family. Attention was also possible because of subscriptions paid by parishes or as a result of donations received by the hospital.

The Horton was well served by its early trustees. Among these were such familiar names as Colonel North MP, Bernhard Samuelson (local industrialist and benefactor) and William Mewburn of Wykham Park.

Over the years that followed the foundation of the Horton money flowed in as well as supplies of materials such as linen, cotton lint and bandages.

In 1897, as part of the local celebrations of Queen Victoria's Diamond Jubilee, a children's ward was built using money given by the Mewburns.

Further developments awaited the restoration of peace in 1918 when a

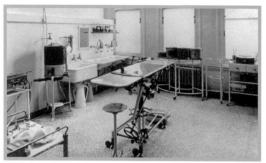
The old operating theatre at the Horton Infirmary.

special memorial fund realised £2,000. This was spent on a nurses' hostel, domestic quarters as well as other new buildings. Some seven years later the men's ward was extended and an electo-therapeutic department was constructed. Patient numbers grew significantly from 285 in 1906 to over 1,000 in 1933.

At the time of the 125th anniversary, an interview with 81-year-old Eric Franklin of Banbury revealed a host of fascinating details about 50 years of change at the Horton. In the 1920s he was a patient, whereas in 1970 Mr Franklin returned as a night nurse.

A verandah at the Horton Infirmary for patients well enough to be outside, or those who were in need of fresh air.

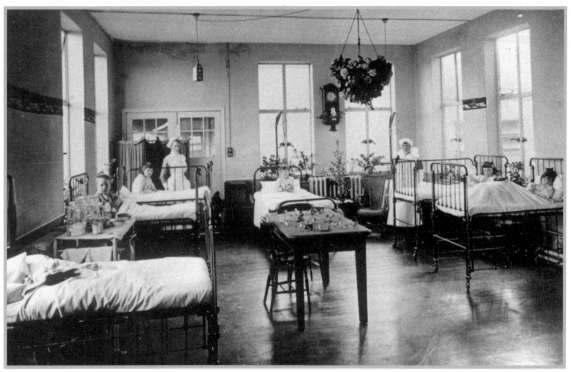

The children's ward at the Horton.

His earlier hospital experience came about as a result of damaging a toe. Because this was non-life threatening it was not long before he moved from inside the men's ward to a veranda. It was from here that Eric was able to view the hospital's carnival procession, which originated from the town and ended up in the field behind the hospital.

His stay at the Horton cost 2d a week. This was stopped from his earnings. Fifty years later he found himself as an agency nurse helping to deal with the worst effects of weekend violence after the pubs had closed.

Some idea of the effect of World War Two on the Horton was revealed in a 1997 interview with Jean Charles (née Tyrrell) who was a nurse then. She recalled that they did not have to deal with too many casualties during the night but, at times of bombing, had to carry out their normal duties despite large numbers of people seeking protection within the building. Air wardens trying to get some sleep often occupied trolleys.

Fundraising – Banbury and District Workpeople's Hospital Association

Donations have played a very important part in the development of the hospital. At the heart of this in the early days has been the Banbury and District Workpeople's Association. The weekly contribution scheme started in 1909, and by 1939 there

Mawles (Ironmongers and Agricultural Machinery) donated money to the Banbury & District Workpeople's Hospital Fund on behalf of employees.

were 10,000 members. Between these dates its members raised just over £96,000 for new equipment. They embraced all walks of life but very prominent were people like Captain Snowball of World War One munitions factory fame and Baron Profumo of Avon Dassett.

Leading firms in Banbury played their part as well. The Northern Aluminium Company contributed £375 in 1939 and there were other substantial amounts from Hunt Edmunds, Henry Stone & Son, Spencer Corsets and the Grand Theatre.

Post war developments

Developments since the war show just how far the Horton Hospital has come from its cottage hospital roots. New buildings have appeared all over the campus, and the active medical and surgical heart is now behind the historic Victorian infirmary. Today's capabilities are especially well revealed by the Accident and Emergency Unit opened in 1989 at a cost £600,000, much of it raised by the public in just over 14 months, largely due to the

tireless efforts of Jack Friswell. The 1994 scanner appeal enjoyed similar success with the £560,000 target being reached in under a year, again with Jack Friswell as chair. More recently a cancer centre has been funded by public subscription.

Another very important aspect of progress has been the evolution of the Rowan Day Hospital founded in 1990. One of its key functions has been to help patients to cope with the non-medical problems of old age.

Elsewhere on site, a feature of the maternity hospital has been the special care baby unit. The opening of the new maternity hospital in 1961 marked the end of an era in which mothers and babies occupied the Elms and the Neithrop Hospital, a former workhouse. If the mother had to have a Caesarean then Sister Eilish Houlihan would take her to the theatre then accompany mother and baby back to Norris Ward.

Christmas at the Horton

Every effort was made to make Christmas

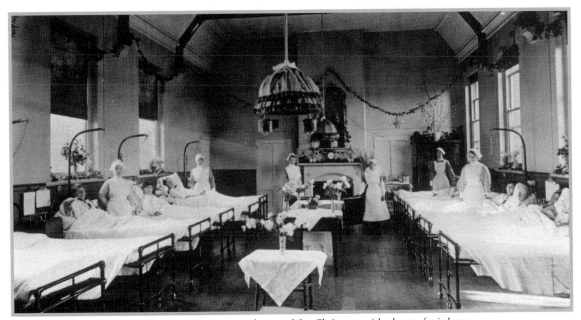

A typical 'Florence Nightingale' ward at the Horton, decorated for Christmas with plenty of mistletoe.

Dr Griffith serves Christmas pudding with some medicinal brandy.

a special time for those who had to remain in hospital. Traditionally, Lord North of Wroxton supplied the tree to the Horton

Infirmary and Mr Bustin, whose electrical business was near to the Cross, illuminated it. Major Edmondson, Banbury's MP, gave gifts and visited the wards, usually accompanied by the Mayor of the day. On Christmas Eve nurses, dressed in their uniform cloaks, sang carols around the wards.

Sister Houlihan, in common with contemporary consultants and surgeons, has many happy memories of Christmas time at the Horton back in the 1960s. Senior staff members like Malcolm Gate, Consultant Gynaecologist, would dress up in various festive costumes and carve the turkey for the noon dinner.

Sisters had their own seasonal dinner in nearby Penrose House. Invariably, the

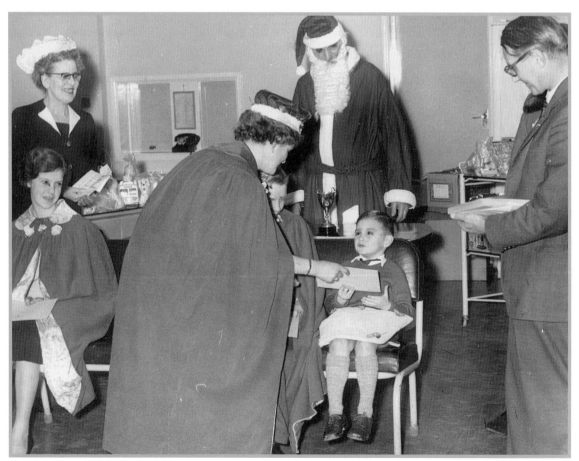

'Auntie Margaret' of the *Banbury Guardian* accompanied by Ted Clark, on the right, distributing gifts to children in hospital over Christmas. In the *Banbury Guardian* issue for Thursday 26 December 1957, 'Auntie Margaret' wrote in the 'Chums Column' about the visit to the Horton by Wendy-Soo (a dog) and herself.

Horton nurses enjoying their Christmas party.

Brownie Lay Band provided the music for this great social occasion.

Battle for survival

In recent years the Horton Hospital has been at the centre of a battle for the survival of services locally. People have taken to the streets when necessary. A familiar 1990s sight was a sea of placards with slogans such as 'Please save our hospital'. Now that it is part of the Oxford Radcliffe Hospitals NHS Trust, prioritising of funding and resource basing has been inevitable. Within this power struggle a new victim may well be paediatrics but not if that inveterate campaigner George Parish can do anything about it.

BANBURY AND THE TWO WORLD WARS

It was in 1913 that the arrival of new council houses gave a hint of developments to come, but one of the most significant effects of World War One was to cause delays in public sector activities pending the return to civilian life of key officers of the Borough such as surveyor Sidney Hilton.

A highly significant and adverse impact of World War One upon the economy of the area was the loss of manpower that was particularly hard on small companies such as Cheneys the printers. Newspapers were also deprived of staff.

Ironically, just as men were leaving the town for the battlefront so some businesses were accumulating war-related work. Printing firms especially benefited, and Cheneys had to give priority to a mass of jobs that came their way from the National

1910 – the Oxfordshire Hussars on their way to Cowley line up near the Cross.

World War One – troops assemble in the Horse Fair.

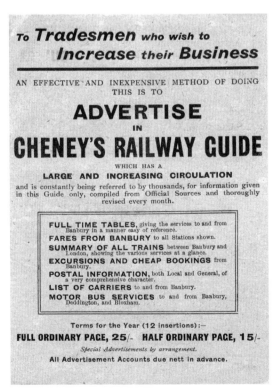

Cheney's Railway Guide for 1916. The guide was published throughout the war but shortage of paper led to a doubling of the price.

Filling Factory in Grimsbury and from the Admiralty whose needs were more complex. These contracts meant access to paper issued under special circumstances. This was especially fortunate as the trade depression of 1914 and 1915 severely strained the company's resources. It did not help matters that partners Daniel Fowler and Fred Robinson both left to work at the munitions factory.

A remarkable aspect of wartime activity at Cheneys was the continuity of production of the famous railway timetables, which were still published in full despite restrictions on dissemination of information generally. The worst that happened to the railway guide was that it doubled in price form 1d to 2d in 1917. In Cheneys own words the timetable was 'an effective and inexpensive method of increasing business for tradesmen'.

Banbury station – Men and horses of the Oxfordshire Light Infantry go off to World War One.

The National Filling Factory

The National Filling Factory, which had such a notable effect on the workload of the likes of Cheneys, came to be located in Banbury because this part of the country was regarded as a safe haven. It could be found midway between Grimsbury and Overthorpe. A network of rails provided access to the London and the North Western line that terminated at Merton Street station. Spread across 248 acres of land by 1917, this factory gave employment to 933 men and 548 women at the peak of its productive activity.

Work was all about filling shells and this attracted the attention of local newspapers with the result that slogans appeared such as:

> Shells, shells and more shells, come and help fill them.
>
> The shell you fill may sink the submarine that sank the *Lusitania*.

The response in the factory was so great that in the week ending 3 March 1917 some 7,000 of the 9.2in (235mm) shells became ready for use. Occasionally a shell would be the means by which a personal message was conveyed to the front. Many such expressions elicited responses and occasionally souvenirs.

Powders used to fill shells had to be treated with great respect. They could cause irritation but more commonly discoloured skin. Handling of them took place in yellow rooms and the women workers became known as 'canaries'.

Production line activity was shift work, for which the average pay was 25s 9d (£1.29) per week. Those on nights could earn 30s 3d (£1.51) and there were bonuses of between 3s (15p) and 16s (80p) a week for additional production. If special powders were required the women were paid an extra 2s (10p), and during each shift a cup of hot cocoa or milk was provided.

The factory, which was managed by a man with the wonderful name of Captain Snowball, was not without its social side. In 1917 a recreational club was formed and the range of sports included tennis, cricket, football and the ever-popular billiards.

Closure of the Grimsbury site did not happen until 1924 but before then employment levels fell considerably once peace had been declared. A general stripping down of plant and machinery took place between 1919 and 1939 but, in spite of German suspicions, there was no revival of the factory during World War Two.

The Red Cross Hospital in Grimsbury

Between 1915 and 1919 a Red Cross Hospital was located in the old Methodist Chapel in West Street. Here injured service personnel were treated after being transported from the Great Western Railway Station. Pressure on the accommodation necessitated the erection of terrapin-type huts from where the view was across open pastureland grazed by Stroud cattle.

Be on your guard

Wherever people lived or worked locally during World War One, an important aspect was awareness of how to respond to the new threat of aircraft raids. On 11 February 1915 Mr Wilson, the chief cconstable of the Borough Police, issued a large poster that was displayed in prominent places. It contained regulations, mainly those to do with lighting and its

Red Cross nurses at the GWR station. They had a hospital in Grimsbury that was largely supported by voluntary contributions.

reduction in intensity or elimination. Banbury's extensive rail sidings would have been operating with greatly reduced amounts of light.

The other main message to people was that the appearance of hostile aircraft would be signalled by a series of short blasts of five seconds duration with five-second intervals between each blast sounded on the Samuelson Work's hooters. In the event of such a warning people were advised to take refuge in cellars and basements, an interesting contrast with the Morrison and Anderson shelters of World War Two.

World War One produced a number of stories that enlivened the pages of the *Banbury Guardian* that was otherwise dominated by the stresses of the time. In February 1915 the inappropriately named Corporal Luck, together with two friends who were privates, had their boots taken by another soldier who passed them on to a Cherwell Terrace chimney sweep. The

sweep was fined £5 for being in receipt of stolen goods.

Peace celebrations

When the war was finally over Banbury celebrated with joyous scenes in the streets, 12 November 1918 was declared a public holiday locally and business throughout the town was suspended and

Robert Kiteley Higham (coal merchant) on his way to the peace celebration at the end of World War One.

shops closed. More enduring were longer-term symbols of relief at the ending of hostilities. A pair of 'peace' cottages were erected in Park Road and an enlarged

Banbury Home Guard in the 1940s.

People's Park was officially opened in 1919 by Lord North of Wroxton Abbey, who was High Steward of Banbury.

World War Two

During World War Two Banbury was regarded as a relatively safe place in which to live. Attacks on the town by enemy aircraft were few in number and most of the small amount of damage was a result of raiders releasing their few remaining bombs following major onslaughts on towns such as Coventry. The Great Western Railway and the nearby gasworks were the prime local targets.

Once again the main problem for the town was how to carry on with reduced manpower. There was a great dependence on women and this was as true of the market stalls as it was on the production lines of the Northern Aluminium Company.

There were special problems relating to the operation of the Merton Street Livestock Market. Restrictions on cattle movements meant that only cattle from within a 10-mile radius of Banbury could

Norman Blinkhorn's works pass for the Northern Aluminium Company. He was responsible for some very important war work.

be handled locally. The town was not the centre of a main grazing area for the fat cattle that had been nine tenths of the trade.

The Northern Aluminium Company – a Banbury firm in wartime

A management statement that appeared in a special issue of the in-house magazine called *Safety First* can gauge the extent of the war effort by those employed at the Southam Road works of the NAC. In this E.L. Ashley said with obvious pride 'we played no small part in the defence of our country during the critical days of the Battle of Britain... and helped to make

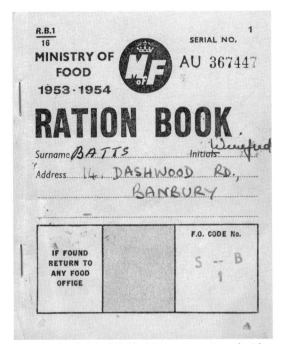

A Ration Book: Mrs Winifred Batts was registered with local retailers Fowlers for meat and Dossett for groceries.

Northern Aluminium Co, women replace men who have been called up for active service.

possible the mighty offensive action... by the Royal Air Force against German industries which hastened the end of the war.' He then added that the role of women working for NAC was crucial as

indeed was the part played by Defence and ARP services in factory security.

At the outset of the war some 240 employees left the works because they

Northern Aluminium Co Home Guard.

were Reservists or Territorials. With metal urgently needed for aircraft the only answer was to work a seven-day week over a prolonged period of time. Buildings were camouflaged as a means of deceiving the enemy and a dummy factory was build further up Hardwick Hill.

Replacement labour was also essential to the war effort. Men above conscription age were drafted in from non-essential occupations such as shop assistants, hairdressers, bus conductors and printers. Increasing numbers of women were recruited, and both they and the men were bussed in from distances of up to 20 miles on a substantial number of buses.

An important spare-time activity was the training of personnel to become members of the Home Guard, National Fire Service, British Red Cross and St John Ambulance Brigade.

It was in May 1940 that the NAC contingent of the Home Guard was formed, and by October its size had increased to over 100 men. There was a Lewis Gun site at the Bourton dummy factory and later guards were mounted at the actual works and also at Switchgear and Equipment premises.

In 1941 the company was absorbed within the Banbury Battalion and defence of the works was extended to defence of the town. At peak strength the NAC Home Guard numbered 256, a figure that was allowed to decline from the end of 1944.

Another, and important, way in which employees helped in the war effort was through a National Savings Group. There were four special weeks – War Weapons, Warships, Wings for Victory and Salute the Soldier. The combined total collected

over these four weeks was in excess of £30,000.

Victory celebrations

On Tuesday 8 May 1945 the nation celebrated the end of the war against Hitler and his European allies (VE Day). At 3.00pm a huge crowd appeared outside Banbury Town Hall where they heard Winston Churchill's address to the nation relayed by loud speakers. After this broadcast the Mayor of Banbury, Alderman Mascord, echoed Churchill's speech when in a call to action he said 'Go away and, according to your desires, be joyful'. Sadly it was not a joyous occasion for all as there were a number with family involvement in the continuing hostilities in the Far Eastern theatre of war. They had to wait for VJ Day and the return of those Japanese prisoners of war who survived the conflict.

In common with previous periods of celebration such as the Silver Jubilee of George V in 1935 and the Coronation of George VI in 1937, certain parts of the town made outstanding contributions to VE Day festivities.

People of the Cherwell district were expected to 'come out with an amazing show'. Undoubtedly, the especially close-knit nature of its communities had something to do with this.

Calthorpe Street and parts of Neithrop were determined not to be outdone and it was reported in the local newspapers that residents in some streets had been paying into a club in order to meet the cost of flags and materials for decoration.

Businessmen and firms entered into the spirit of the occasion. Norman Blinkhorn of the South Bar photographic studios

VE Day 1945 celebrated in the playground of Dashwood Road School.

added floodlighting to the fine trees on the approaches to the Cross. The Braggins family of timber merchants placed a massive 'V for Victory' sign at the top of a tall crane in Gatteridge Street.

All these preparations for VE Day would have meant a lot to people who remembered the town of the 1930s, but it is also interesting to gauge the reactions of children. A newspaper reporter asked a happy youngster from the Grimsbury area what he thought of it all. Back came the response, 'All right so long as we don't have to write a composition about it'.

During the following weeks street parties could be found in almost every part of the town. At each of these, teatime goodies made from carefully hoarded rations of sugar and fats spread across trestle tables and people danced to recorded music provided by Albert Boote and his Banbury Sound. Whenever possible the Mayor and Mayoress attended these and left with gifts to mark the occasion. Sheila Robinson of Upper Windsor Street was a mere two years old when she handed a bouquet to the civic couple.

Just as the tempo of events appeared to be winding down, a victory Fun Fair opened on Easington Recreation Ground. Hard times lay ahead, but during the war people had learnt to live for the moment and enjoy what they had.

Crowds at Banbury Fair in Edwardian times. Note the Post Office at the top left.

FAIRS AND MARKETS

Since mediaeval times Banbury has had a well-established tradition for the association of particular products such as wool and cheese with certain periods of the year. These specialised markets were known as fairs. For instance, in the 16th century Thursday 28 February was Fish Fair day while Thursday 3 January became known as the Leather Fair. At the outset of the 17th century the present street known as Horse Fair was emerging from its earlier designation of Horse Market, probably because it was here that the Twelfth or Horse Fair was located.

At the beginning of the 20th century the only fairs remaining were the January Horse Fair or Twelfth Day Fair (normally the first Thursday after the old Twelfth Day, somewhere around the 25 January), a further horse fair on the third Thursday in September and the Michaelmas hiring fair in mid October.

In the 19th and early 20th centuries the Twelfth Fair was held in the space between the Cross and what is now the Church House Bistro. It was eagerly awaited by dealers and tenant farmers especially and extended over four days. If you wanted a quality horse then atten-

dance on the first two days was essential. During the third day available animals were of a lower order and on the final day the emphasis was on cheap horses and donkeys (so called Gipsy Day). Horses were either sold privately, mostly in the Horse Fair but occasionally in other parts of the town such as a canal wharf, or by auction.

A highlight of the four-day event was the organisation within rings of a series of competitions for the local tenant farmers. If numbers taking part were very large then additional ring space had to be sought elsewhere such as on the Marshes beyond the present day Castle Street.

This fair reached the height of its importance in about 1900. In the present day the nearest equivalents are the annual Horse Fairs at Stow on the Wold and at Appleby in north-west England.

In the late 19th century the Michaelmas Fair was still the peak of Banbury's trading and recreational year. Sales of cattle and cheese with which it was originally associated had gone, but the farmers still used the opportunity to trade grain and engage labour. Such was its renown that the vast crowds included farmers

Stalls and booths in front of the Town Hall in the 1950s.

Banbury Fair in the
Market Place *c.*1904.

from the north hoping to engage farm workers at the hiring fair and the army looking for recruits. Those seeking work, who assembled mostly in Parsons Street, wore badges of trades. Maidservants no longer stood with labourers in the street as they had in the 17th century but occupied indoor rooms. However, most noticeable was the growing importance of the pleasure fair.

Anyone who lived in the Middleton Road area of Grimsbury before World War One would have been more aware of the onset of fair activities than most people living in either Banbury or Grimsbury today. Showmen's caravans arrived on land behind the Cricketers Inn, an area known as the 'Slinkett'.

On the Sunday prior to the setting up of the rides and sideshows, ladies from these caravans dressed in their best clothes went to worship at St Leonard's Church. Immediately prior to the three days of the Michaelmas Fair those responsible for the various entertainments and rides walked in procession from where they were parked by way of the bridge to the Cow Fair.

Many of those people whose recollections go back as far as the 1920s have spoken enthusiastically of an instantaneous experience, a magical kind of fairyland generated by the mass of light. The sound of hurdy-gurdy music and the sight of fairgoers ambling about clutching their bags of Needle's fish and chips were an added dimension.

Often young children had only a few pennies available but cast eager eyes on the mammoth switchback in front of the Town Hall or the nearby galloping horses. Lots of sideshows claimed attention, notably the Fat Lady and the boxing booth that was always situated close to the Prudential Buildings in the Market Place.

At the end of the evening it was customary to go home with a fairing – a memento of the visit. This might be a cheap ornament, some Banbury Cakes or even a bag of brandy snaps. One person for whom the duration of the fair could not be too long was Muriel Herbert, who as a child lived in Grimsbury in the 1920s. In her words, 'on Saturday I ventured somewhat tentatively as far as the Albion (an inn on the Banbury side of the bridge) hoping against hope that the sights and sounds would still be visible and audible. Rational thinking ruled otherwise but the journey was compelling – ah the magic of the fair!'

A very special kind of magic accompanied the fair of 1922. The *Banbury Guardian* printed a small advertisement that read 'don't miss seeing the Johnson Family of Lady Swimmers'. It seems that the performance was all about their eating, sleeping, sewing and writing under water. This series of feats of endurance was a first for Banbury people.

In 1931, encouraged by especially fine weather, thousands of people visited the attractions and there was an almost complete absence of drunkenness and rowdyism. For the first time in its history the three-day event did not have to contend with market livestock wandering the streets; memories of the occasion were not of confrontations with store cattle but of the very popular ghost train and motor carnival dodgems in Cornhill.

Three years later a thrilling new attraction was the airways roundabout (chair-o-plane). This novelty combined swing with

A young Johnny Biddle at the ever-popular coconut shy.

Motorcyclists performed spectacular rides, sometimes with passengers, usually pretty girls, who performed acrobatics on the pillion seat or handlebars.' She goes on to observe that 'young men queued up at the shooting gallery to impress their girl-friends with their prowess.' Post-war rides became more sophisticated and the Waltzer replaced the chair-o-planes. There is no doubt that in recent times the trend towards greater thrills has become very apparent. Significantly, Bob Wilson's poster for 2004 featured two people with their hair standing on end. In the *Banbury Guardian* issue of 23 October 1947 the reporter of the day posed the question, 'What are the chances of queuing outside the Town Hall for a five minute trip to the moon from Banbury Fair?' The answer then was virtually nil. Not so in the 21st century with sensations such as the reverse bungee jump.

up and down motion. Above all fairgoers had an extra hour in which to enjoy all the fun of the fair. Shutdown was not until 11.45pm.

Someone else who found Banbury Fair a wondrous occasion was June Hardie, a former North Newington resident who came to town regularly. She has recalled the fair both before and just after World War Two. 'Rides were nothing like the technical wonders of today. One great attraction was the Wall of Death.

Fairground families, typical of those who brought their shows to Banbury.

A person whose recollections come straight out of the world of showmen is Johnny Biddle. He had an aunt, Nanny Curtis, who ran a sweet stall, with local rock a speciality. This was drawn out on a great hook and changed colour in the process. She had a pitch in Bridge Street and was one of the caravan dwellers parked behind the Cricketers in Grimsbury.

Many past shows at the Michaelmas Fair have been linked to people who became personalities in their own right. Until the 1960s Lady Buckland was always associated with the coconut shy. Another familiar figure was Billy Lee with his Kentucky Derby racehorses. These operated around a circuit and you bought a ticket, which was your golden gamble. Both these show how originality was the making of Banbury Fair. It was a prime reason why local people looked forward to the three days of entertainment.

Showmen aside, enjoyment of the fair meant different things to different people. There were those for whom no visit was complete without a plate of whelks, whereas others took away memories of encounters with those such as the Turpin brothers at Gage's boxing booth in the Market Place.

On the Thursday (second night) of the fair, it was always customary to hold a dance at the Town Hall for show people, their families and friends. Many stalls used to close down earlier than usual so that this special occasion could be enjoyed to the full. The last ever dance of this kind was held at the General Foods Social Club in the early 1970s.

At the very end of the Fair, a well-established tradition was an ox roast in the yard of the Crown in Bridge Street. Prime movers in its organisation were the Masons, family butchers who had a nearby, popular shop. They would endeavour to get the mayor of the day to cut the first slice.

In one sense the annual layout of the fair shows and amusements owes much to the way Banbury's street pattern evolved in mediaeval times. The large space in front of the Town Hall, known originally as the Cow Fair, has always been regarded as the 'prime pitch' for the most attractive piece of equipment.

With increasing pressure on available central area spaces, the present day fair has had to sacrifice consolidation for continuity and has found new locations such as spaces near the Cross where the pre-1925 sheep market used to attract numerous buyers and sellers.

Doubts about the future of the street fair have been raised long and often. Such was the crush of people in the early years of the 20th century that shop windows had to be boarded up with subsequent loss of trade. Sometimes these doubts have been allied to remarks like 'not as good as in previous years'. For instance, in 1955 the *Banbury Guardian* noted that 'the fair appeared thinner than usual'. However, its family organisers were determined not to go under. Typical was the spirited talk to Rotarians in October 1955, which was given by Robert (Bob) Wilson. His punch line was uncompromising, 'I have been told that there are some who are trying to do away with Banbury Fair. I would like those men to know that while I am alive I will fight them.' The sincerity of this remark was matched by an advertisement in the *Banbury Guardian* that referred to

1999 was the first year part of the Fair was moved to the Horse Fair after the old bus station made way for Castle Quay.

that year's event as 'Old Banbury Pleasure Fair'.

The Produce Market

The produce market of the 1930s was very different from that of the present day. Then traders owned their own stalls and were committed to longer hours. Some remained open until 9.00pm in winter and 10 o'clock in summer. Illuminated by naptha flares, the Market Place came alive after dark when crowds of people sought bargains. Rhoda Woodward, quoted in a *Banbury Guardian* issue of 1996, commented that late purchases could often be profitable. Her father once returned home from the market bearing a carrier full of fruit for which he had paid 6d (2p).

Outside Mawditt's cake shop at the eastern end of the Market Place there was a hog market from which, from time to time, pigs escaped to cause mayhem among the stalls. Other forms of livestock contributed to the character of this area and included wire cages piled on top of each other full of hens, rabbits and the odd ferret. At certain times of the year there would also be day-old chicks and ducklings, and at Christmas time it was not uncommon to see 50-strong flocks of turkeys that had been walked into Banbury from nearby villages like North Newington.

Between the wars many stalls were operated by true personalities. Outstanding among them was Rocky Leach, a large man renowned for his Banbury rock made in a profusion of colours and flavours.

Jack Spencer was also well known to all. He brought stockings, socks and

The Produce Market fills
the Market Place, *c.*1920.

Rocky Leach by his stall in Banbury Market.

underwear from his home city of Leicester. Competing with him were the Peacocks, whose stall also offered work to several local girls.

Certain owners of shops located around the Market Place also sold goods in the market, such as Salmons, who were confectioners and who had a retail shop on the north side. Wyncolls were initially known for their banana stall and then took the opportunity to diversify into fruit, flowers and vegetables in a North Bar shop. Certain of the Market Place, businesses like Nathans used to create pavement displays so as to challenge the supremacy of the market stall owners and prevent them from encroaching too close to the lock-up shops.

In 1999 Jim Hargan came to Banbury from the Smoky Mountains region of the US and was especially impressed by the bi-weekly market. A photographer and writer, he decided to record his memories in an American travel magazine entitled *British Heritage*. The article was entitled 'the Markets of Banbury', and in it Jim observed that 'by seven in the morning queues formed in front of the produce stands; housewives shout their orders while attendants lean over stacks of vegetables to reach them.' To his amazement and in his words 'by four the Market Place is a municipal parking lot again.'

It was about the time of Jim Hagan's visit that an August event known as 'Great British Market Week' was bringing out the bunting on at least some of the stalls. However, all was not well as rental increases on top of earlier rises were dampening spirits and restricting profits. Interviews with some traders and shoppers created the impression that Banbury market had lost some of its charm and lacked the bustle and variety of somewhere like Oakham in Leicestershire. In part this was due to a declining number of personalities like Alfie with his clock and watch pitch near the entrance to Parsons Street and an incessant cry of "'alf price in the sale today ladies'. An article in a 1994 issue of the *Banbury Guardian* focussed on a remarkable lady who became the first female chairperson of the Banbury Branch of the Market Traders' Association. Sylvia Sawdon was a stall-holder by chance. Returning after a holiday, she decided to take on the haberdashery business previously run by her former husband.

Concerns about the Thursday and Saturday markets have continued beyond the Millennium. Since Christmas 2003 there has been growing worry about the control and composition of these markets. This relates especially to the belief that the Banburyness of our town is at least in part somehow dependent on the persistence of time-hallowed activities within their traditional surroundings. The twice-weekly gathering of stalls draws much of its attraction from a setting that in some towns is being radically altered in the name of regeneration. The importance of the whole issue was highlighted in a *Banbury Guardian* article that appeared beneath the heading 'Banbury speaks its Mind'.

Matters came to a head in 2004 when Cherwell District Council gave control of the market to Hughmark International, a Reading-based firm with relevant experience. Since this change of ownership advertisements have appeared in the local press designed to encourage new participants in the operation of a 12th-century institution.

The WI Stall

Since 1919 Women's Institute stalls have appeared in weekly markets across the country. However, it was not until 1934 that one appeared at Banbury market and then in the wake of a successful enterprise in Oxford. The *Banbury Guardian,* in its issue of 22 March, carried the news 'Oxfordshire Women's Institutes have completed their arrangements for a market stall which will be in Banbury

Miss Rogers at the WI stall in 1937.

market every Saturday from 7 April'. The article went on to identify a wide range of items for sale – poultry, eggs, cream, jam, cakes, fruit and vegetables.

Visitors to the very first stall, opened by Banbury's mayor James Friswell, would have encountered the Hon Mrs Bathurst (treasurer of the Oxfordshire federation of WIs), Miss Rogers of London (stall controller) and Miss Merchant of

Today's WI stall in Cornhill with its wide range of produce. Left to right: John Anson, Pandy Fox, Linda Herring and Jen Taylor.

Somerton (cashier). Miss Rogers was a redoubtable figure in her long, white coat and bucket hat. They had before them a tempting array as diverse as dressed fowl and chutney. The hope was to equal the weekly takings in Oxford, which amounted to some £40.

During the 1950s turnover on the stall see-sawed and WI members needed reminding that sales of produce should be encouraged whenever the opportunity occurred.

The 1930s stall was located outside a popular refreshment venue called the Apple Tree Tea Rooms, and not Cornhill where it can be found today. Last year yet another milestone was reached, the 70th anniversary. Judging by the crowds that flock to the stall each Saturday, come rain or shine, it appears likely to retain its place.

The Farmers' Market

A recent popular feature to enliven Banbury's Market Place has been the monthly Farmers' Market. Comprising a dozen or so stalls, this has come to occupy the Cornhill enclave during the morning of the first Friday of every month.

Underneath the gaily coloured awnings are pigs roasting on spits, sausages filled with meat from the likes of wild boar, all manner of breads, cheeses, eggs, honeys, plants, fruit and vegetables and even British wines from a local vineyard. Purveyors of all these come from a 20-mile radius of Banbury, and all can claim that their products follow a direct route from the farm to the customer.

Unlike the charter and statutory markets of Thursday and Saturday, the farmers' market is all but over by

A pig roast at the Farmers' Market.

lunchtime. Since the Banbury market started, a second and alternative Farmers' Market has sprung up at Deddington, just south of Banbury, and people throng to it on those Saturdays when stalls fill the old Market Place.

The Cattle Market

At the beginning of the 20th century the buying and selling of animals took place in the streets as it had done down the centuries, and many of the street names in Banbury reflect this. Cattle were always to be found in the Cow Fair (the part of Bridge Street in front of the Town Hall) and the lower High Street or Beastmarket, whereas sheep were penned on the eastern side of the Horse Fair having been moved there from the part of the upper High Street that was formerly called Sheep Street.

In the Cow Fair and Beast Market cattle were marshalled or tethered prior to sales outside the nearby inns such as the White Hart. The Cow Fair was also a thoroughfare for animal movements and for farmers in carts with their churns of milk for the nearby produce market.

Up until the 1940s Bridge Street had a life all of its own. Unlike today some people resided in this part of the town centre. Typical was the family of Raymond Bernard Miller who was company secretary to Hunt Edmunds Brewery for some 25 years. The Millers lived in a large house called Havenfield that backed on to the brewery's builders yard. In the 1920s the Thursday cattle market was very adjacent, so much so that a slightly raised footpath in front of the house was the sole means of keeping livestock at a distance. Come the end of the

The bottom end of the High Street where Farmers and Dealers met at the beginning of the 20th century.

Sheep pens being set out for the Thursday sheep market.

day and there was the sight of men cleaning up the mess. It seems that their efforts were less vigorous than those of the stockmen.

Until 1901 there was a small hog market with provision for fur and feather sales outside the Angel public house in the north-east corner of the Market Place.

That year the Superintendent of Police closed down the pig area because of the possibility of swine fever.

Norman Scroxton, one of the best-remembered headmasters in the town, recalled youthful experiences in pre-1914 Banbury. The part of the Horse Fair close to the Cross was an occasional play area. Here on Wednesday evenings hurdles were put in place for Thursday's sheep sales. These were a good test of athletic prowess as indeed were the more permanent iron railings that lined Bridge and Broad Streets. Actual market day transformation of this Horse Fair area can be gauged from a booklet, *memories around Edge Hill 1922–1939*, by Terry Steatham. In this, he recalls taking sheep to market in Banbury. 'On arrival…, after jogging along the roads through Edge Hill and Wroxton, we… unloaded our sheep into sheep pens, then fed and watered the horses. Often the men had a shilling available to buy some sweets or a bar of Nestlé's chocolate for mum and a packet of five Woodbines for dad.'

By 1923, due to limited space, part of Broad Street had had to be incorporated and as this was not universally popular an alternative scheme was mooted. This involved utilising some spare capacity in the sheep market for cattle sales.

Medical recommendations of the day pointed to the desirability of a new style location for the whole livestock marketing operation. Persistence in the use of streets was considered 'injurious to the health and well-being of the community'.

In March 1923 members of Banbury Borough Council met to consider a submission by a syndicate of unnamed people who wanted to trade on private

ground. By a margin of just one vote the council decided to licence this syndicate. This brought about a strong reaction in the local Press to the effect that more public involvement in any decision about the future of the market was desirable. Editorials contained comments about balancing the views of dealers, farmers, shopkeepers and burgesses (voters).

In the event, a syndicate did take over responsibility for market arrangements but not at the location close to the Warwick Road/Coventry Road junction favoured by the Council. The syndicate's preferred site was on private and council-owned space adjacent to the London and North Western Railway in Grimsbury. It was here that the company Midland Marts Limited took root and facilitated sales of livestock from around 1925 until the market's closure in mid-1998.

During the early years the Chamber of Trade monitored developments, mainly because of shopkeepers' concerns about the loss of sales caused by farmers making fewer visits to the main retail streets that were in Banbury town centre and not Grimsbury. Their fears gradually disappeared as it became clear that those who used the new consolidated market still needed the goods and services on which they had always depended. If there was a problem it was more to do with closures of popular licensed premises such as the Red Lion and the Old George where farmers had enjoyed a drink or two and a market ordinary (lunch).

The Christmas Fat Stock Show
For most of the years covered by this book, the Fat Stock Show has been an

event of considerable importance in Banbury's December calendar. Until the mid-1920s this was still very much a street-orientated occasion. Cattle were exhibited in the Cow Fair (in front of the Town Hall), sheep in the Horse Fair and poultry and butter at the Vine in Cornhill. Judges and officials used to turn the show into a social occasion by gathering for lunch at the Red Lion in the High Street. The show of 1976 held at the cattle market had a very special outcome; a prize-winning heifer was purchased by the Manor Hotel in the Oxford Road for the then record price of £1,000.

Midlands Marts' Banbury Stockyard

Visitors to the Merton Street area of Grimsbury used to come across a large sign with information about day-by-day variations in livestock movements. Until very recently it was the only evidence of

PRICE — SIXPENCE

THE SIXTY-FIFTH
Banbury Christmas
FAT STOCK SHOW

WEDNESDAY, DECEMBER 11th, 1957
SALE ON THURSDAY, DECEMBER 12th, 1957
Commencing at 12 (mid-day)
At MIDLAND MARTS SALEYARD
Judging 10 o'clock a.m.

Official List of Entries

President : R. A. BUDGETT, Esq., M.F.H.

Secretary : Mr. G. F. RILEY

Hon. Treasurer : Mr. W. WILLIAMS

Office : SALEYARD

COMMITTEE :
Mr. R. S. Lidsey (Chairman)
Messrs. G. Gibbard, J. Stevens, W. Paxman, M. Passmore, T. S. Pike,
K. Gibbard, A. P. McDougall, W. J. Fowler, S. B. Young, R. G.
Tustian, C. R. Adams, G. Woolgrove, S. J. Gage, R. F. Colegrave,
A. J. Woolgrove, W. Williams, F. T. Kieldsen, S. Peckover, L. J. Pickett,
W. Rathbone and Dudley Beck.

List of entries for the 65th Banbury Christmas Fat Stock Show in 1957.

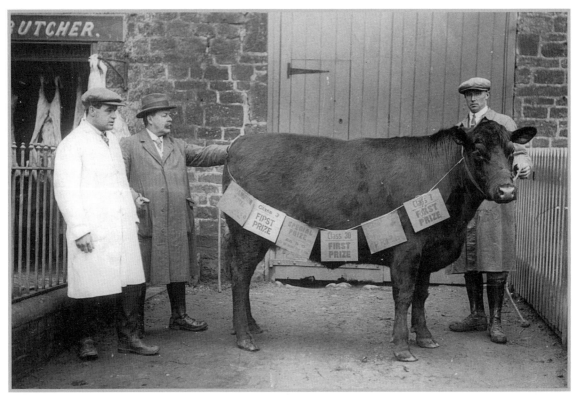

Jarvis Butchers, Middleton Cheney, with prize animals bought at Banbury Market.

A typical busy sale ring scene at the Livestock Market.

the nearby market that was controlled by Midland Marts.

The business was always known as the Banbury Stockyard and enjoyed a high profile status within this country and throughout Europe. This was echoed in issues of a weekly pamphlet, *Midland Marts' Sales News*. Typical promotional slogans were 'Banbury Buying Power' and 'We lead, others follow'. The

Tony Phipps pushes out the pigs at the Midlands Marts Livestock Market.

true meaning of these was reflected in live-stock sales for February 1990 when figures in excess of £600 were paid by Pearson and Sons of Towcester and by P. Gibbs based at Shenington for cows and heifers.

At that time typical enterprise on the part of Midland Marts included the organisation of visits to countries in Europe in order to increase awareness of farming and carry the market flag of Banbury into areas of potential business. In early May 1990 there was a five-day trip to France for all sheep vendors at the Banbury Stockyard. The main thrust of this visit was to sample sheep farming in the Limoges area and to experience the

Rungis Meat Market in Paris at 5.00am. In June 1998 Banbury Stockyard closed very suddenly. It was the end of an era that had commenced with the transfer of live-stock sales from the streets and open spaces of the town to the single site in Grimsbury. For a brief while in 1998 there was the prospect of a new stockyard development at Huscote Farm on the outskirts of Grimsbury but crucially as it turned out in South Northamptonshire. There was a great deal of opposition from the South Northants District Council who viewed the proposals as being on the 'wrong side' of the M40 motorway and setting a precedent for 'further sprawl into a rural area'.

Empty pens at Midland Marts Stockyard – no more to market. The end of an era at Midlands Marts Stockyard.

TO SEE A FINE LADY

On Wednesday 27 April 2005 HRH the Princess Royal unveiled the long-awaited statue of the 'Lady on the White Horse'. Before doing this the royal visitor remarked 'the statue reflects a very fine piece of art you will be proud of in the future and it reflects the extraordinary fame Banbury has across the world.' She added 'it's so well known for its nursery rhyme'.

Ride a Cock Horse

The fine lady looks towards the town's other two earlier tourist attractions, namely the 1859 Cross and the late 18th-century classical-style Parish Church of St Mary. Neither of these is the original structure on the site as earlier crosses had succumbed to Puritan zeal in 1602 and the 12th-century St Mary's had to be pulled down in 1790, partly as a result of

How most people saw the sculpture in the days before the unveiling.

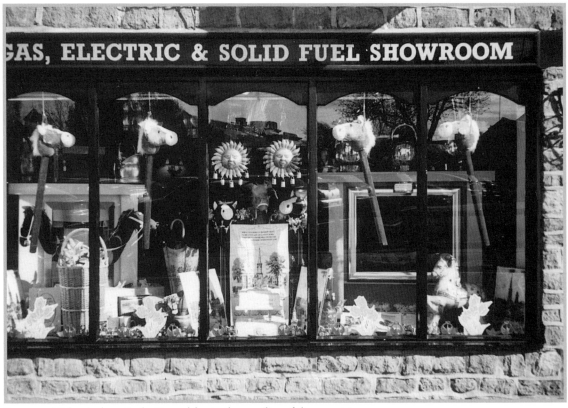

Rosemary Higham's shop, By the Fire, celebrates the unveiling of the new statue.

Part of the 2,000 strong crowd present for the unveiling of the statue on 27 April 2005.

The Lady on the White Horse leads the peace celebrations in 1919.

The Princess Royal with Banbury's Mayor Surinder Dhesi await the presentation of a bouquet by nine-year-old Heather Barlow.

The Artcycle artists responsible for the sculpture, left to right: Andrew Edwards, Carl Payne and Julian Jeffery along with local consultant engineer Andrew Baxter.

Kathleen Harper as the Lady on the White Horse on a much earlier occasion.

damage sustained in the Civil War, which were not properly repaired.

Irrespective of the various theories about the Lady's involvement with May Day celebrations or her links with Coventry's Lady Godiva or Celia Fiennes, a relative of the Fiennes of Broughton Castle (there is no evidence she ever set foot in Broughton Castle or visited Banbury), those severe looking ladies who have re-enacted the part for past pageants and processions have done their bit to keep exciting traditions alive. Certainly the 2,000 or so people who watched the April unveiling must have thought so.

The Lady on the White Horse – the realisation of a dream that was 17 years in the making.

BIBLIOGRAPHY

The titles listed below have been chosen to give readers an opportunity to explore the history of Banbury more fully. Out of print items may be borrowed through local libraries or consulted in the Banburyshire Study Centre of Banbury Library.

General

Allen, Peter *Cherwell Valley Railway: The Social History of an Oxfordshire Railway* (1999).

BHS *Cake & Cockhorse* (hereafter C & Ch), the magazine of the Banbury Historical Society issued to members three times a year.

Beesley, Alfred *The History of Banbury* (1841).

Bloxham, C. *The Book of Banbury* (1975).

Brinkworth, E.R.C. *Old Banbury* (1958).

Clark, Ted *Banbury: History and Guide (1992).*

Herbert, G. *Shoemaker's Window* (1948).

Little, B. *Banbury: A History* (2003).

Little, B. *The Changing Faces of Banbury* (1998).

Little, B. *The Changing Faces of Grimsbury* (1999).

Little, B. and B. Davis *The Changing Faces of Easington* (2000).

Mann, Michael *Workers on the Move* (1973).

Potts, W. *Banbury Through a Hundred Years* (1942).

Potts, W. *A History of Banbury* (1958).

Stacey, Margaret *Tradition and Change: A Study of Banbury* (1960).

Stacey, Margaret, Eric Batstone, Colin Bell and Anne Murcott *Power, Persistence and Change* (1975).

Tempest, E. and B. Kendall *Banbury: A History and Celebration* (2004).

Town Development Group *Banbury Seventy Thousand* (1966).

Trinder, B. *Victorian Banbury* (1982).

Wood, V. *The Licensees of the Inns, Taverns and Beerhouses of Banbury, Oxfordshire* (1998).

Victoria County History of Oxfordshire Vol. X, Ed. Alan Crossley, *Banbury: A History,* reprint for Oxfordshire County Libraries 1984.

INDEX

Numbers in **bold** indicate page references to illustrations